MW00804452

Michigan
Blue-Ribbon
Fly-Fishing Guide

Bob Linsenman

*Gerry and Wes,
This one was fun!

Love Bob*

Michigan

Blue-Ribbon
Fly-Fishing Guide

Bob Linsenman

Frank
Amato
PORTLAND

Dedication
For my sisters—Geraldine, Carlene, and Carol. They have been
unified in their unwavering support, but a bit argumentative
over their nicknames—Nosey, Stinky, and Crabby.

Acknowledgments
Lots of folks provided assistance as I worked on this book, including the guy
in the rusty Jeep who pulled me out of a ditch in remote Baraga county.
More direct and continued help came from Mike Bachelder, Glen
Blackwood, Tom Buhr, Andy Bush, Bob Clark, Kelly Galloup,
John Giuliani, Dawn Kemp, Russ Maddin, Mike Moreau,
Kelly Neuman, John Ramsay, Ray Schmidt, Steve
Sendek, Matt Supinski, Steve Swihart, Chris
Vincent, John Vincent, Karl Vogel,
Kim Koch and Kathy Johnson
of Frank Amato Publications.
My sincere thanks
to you all.

© 2002 Bob Linsenman
ALL RIGHTS RESERVED. No part of this book
may be reproduced by any means without the written
consent of the publisher, except in the case of brief excerpts in
critical reviews and articles. All inquiries should be addressed to:

Frank Amato Publications, Inc.
P.O. Box 82112, Portland, Oregon 97282
503·653·8108 • www.amatobooks.com

All photographs by Bob Linsenman unless otherwise noted.
Fly Plate Photographs: Jim Schollmeyer

Book & Cover Design: Kathy Johnson

Printed in Singapore

Softbound ISBN: 1-57188-160-3   UPC: 0-66066-00358-4
1 3 5 7 9 10 8 6 4 2

Contents

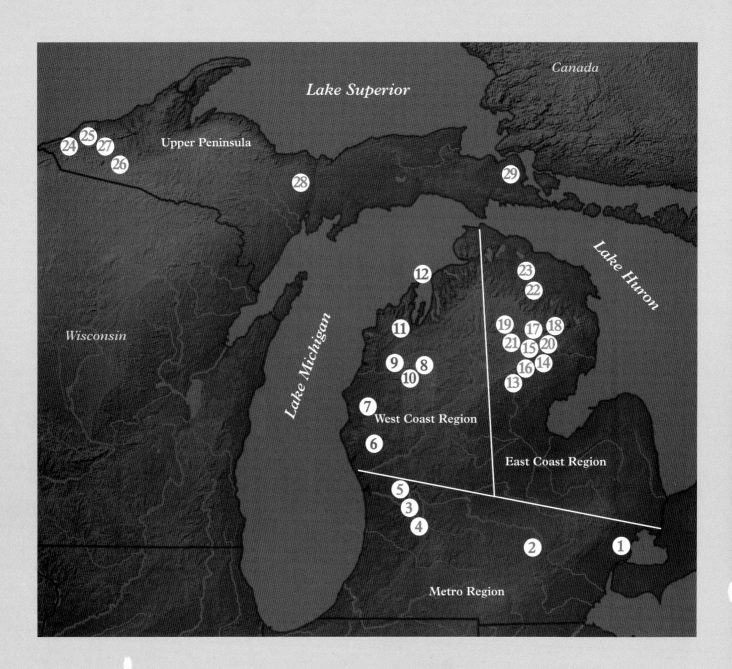

Lake Superior

Canada

Upper Peninsula

㉔ ㉕ ㉗
㉖
㉘
㉙

Wisconsin

Lake Michigan

⑫

⑪

⑨ ⑧
⑩

⑦ West Coast Region

⑥

⑤
③
④

② ①

Lake Huron

㉓
㉒

⑲ ⑰ ⑱
㉑ ⑮ ⑳
⑯ ⑭
⑬

East Coast Region

Metro Region

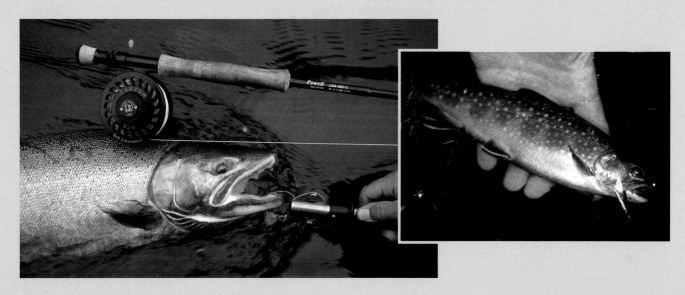

Introduction

The geography and geology of Michigan is unique in all the world. Two peninsulas surrounded by big water define the state—its climate, topography and resources, its history and future. The Great Lakes basin cannot be shown without presenting a clear and precise map of Michigan. Around and through it flows much of the world's supply of fresh water. There is water everywhere. Michigan has more than 11,000 inland lakes, over 30,000 miles of rivers and streams, and the longest coastline of any state excepting Alaska. In fact, Michigan's coastline is longer than either entire seaboard of the west or east coast of the United States.

These classic Au Sable River boats work the Holy Water near Gates' Au Sable Lodge.

I was born and raised here, relocated for work and moved back. While working in New York City and later in Minneapolis, I traveled back to Michigan several times each year. My family was told that I missed them and that was true, but I centered my visits around steelhead runs and major hatches on great rivers. Once I was caught fishing without visiting. A nephew saw me and blew the whistle. Pressure. I sold my house and moved back home to Oscoda County.

It was overwhelming at first; there was so much to do, so many rivers and lakes. Now it is clear that one life is not enough. There are not enough hours in a day, days in a year, years in a lifetime. With this begrudged acknowledgement came a measure of peace. I know I can't be on the Manistee and the Au Sable at the same time, I can't throw poppers to bass on Lake St. Clair and strip streamers for northerns on Hubbard simultaneously. I know this, but I'm restless about it, so it's an uneasy peace.

Most of Michigan's fame as a fly-angling venue centers on trout, salmon and steelhead. This is fair enough. The trout-fishing is outstanding with healthy fish and great rivers—both famous and anonymous. These are complemented by jewel-like inland trout lakes and the shorelines and flats of Superior, Michigan and Huron.

There is much more. Michigan has excellent fly-fishing for bass, panfish, northerns, musky. If it swims in fresh water, it is probably here. Fly-fishing for warmwater species is underexplored on both peninsulas. As such, it offers less pressure (real and imagined) and more solitude. Our bluegills reach 2 pounds, bass often exceed 6 pounds, northerns in the 15- to 20-pound range are numerous, and a musky in the 50-pound range is possible.

As fly-anglers we need to be thinking a bit about

Guide Bob Clark (left) and author with a typical Manistee River steelhead.

Smallmouth bass are a favorite fly-rod quarry throughout Michigan.

spreading the pressure over a wider resource base. Our trout and steelhead rivers can be crowded at times. We might be loving them to death. But this is not a problem on prime water for "other" species, even at peak times. Despite the high and ever-growing number of fly-anglers, I never sense competition or feel crowded while fishing for bluegills, bass or northerns. This fly-fishing is productive and great fun.

What to include? What to eliminate? This was very difficult. I centered on lakes and streams that provide a balance in different regions of the state, that balance attempts to measure quality of fly-fishing with relative ease of access and a sense of solitude. A book of 1,000 pages could not cover all the possibilities.

This may be surprising to some, but the Lower Peninsula (my opinion) has the better fly-angling. There are more cooling springs and aquifers below the Straits of Mackinac. More lakes, more rivers, and more people, of course. So, it was a measure of balance. The Lower Peninsula is closer to more of the population; it's only a five-hour drive from Chicago to the Pere Marquette, for example. But, the Upper Peninsula is a true wilderness experience. It is rugged and beautiful with lonely waters, and loon and wolf serenades. This wilderness is temperamental. The rivers warm quickly and are much more dependent on rain and snow for volume than the streams below the bridge. The lakes, in my experience, can be equally fickle. Still, when they're good, they're unbelievably good.

I had to leave out a lot of fine lakes, ponds, and rivers in the coverage of both peninsulas. This was painful but necessary. The following is but a short list of the excellent fly-fishing water—justifiably "blue-ribbon" that is not included, but should be in your plans.

The West Coast Region

The Kalamazoo, Little Manistee, Boardman, Jordan, Platte, and Betsie rivers, Silver Lake, Torch Lake, Crystal Lake, Spider Lake, Lake Charlevoix.

The East Coast Region

The Maple, Black, Pigeon, and Sturgeon rivers, Burt Lake, Mullett Lake, Shupac Lake, Lake St. Helen, the Lake Huron flats at Singing Bridge.

The Upper Peninsula

The Ontonagon River, Paint River, Huron River, Big Two-Hearted River, Fox River, Escanaba River, Stutts Creek, the flats of Lake Michigan off Thompson, Thousand Island Lake, The Manistique Lakes, Au Train Lake, and all of the Sylvania Recreation Area.

Even this list was difficult to contain. The fact is, we have so much quality water in this state that it is impossible to fish it all. I've been trying hard for over fifty years and now know I'll not be able to fully explore even half.

But, I've cast a lot of flies while wandering and over the years have settled on some favorite lakes and streams. This book contains a few of them.

One thing is for sure, if you cast flies on Michigan waters, you will never be bored.

I
Metro Regions

Many large metropolitan areas have surprisingly good fly-fishing in reasonable proximity to their crowded urban centers. New York has trout streams to the northwest and saltwater opportunities at the doorstep. Minneapolis and St. Paul have numerous lakes and the fine trout streams just a few minutes east at the Wisconsin state line. San Francisco has the bay. Miami, Tampa, Naples, and all of Florida are obvious.

Detroit Area

Chris Vincent holds a nice largemouth from Lake St. Clair. The bass took the author's floating Frog Diver on the first strip.

Detroit is the heart of the nation's manufacturing industry and is regarded as a "factory town." Not many people are aware of the extent and quality of the fly-angling resources within the metro area. The fly-fishing here is good to excellent and (surprisingly) underutilized.

While in college I cut more than a few classes to cast streamers to big rainbow trout in Pine Lake and Orchard Lake to the city's northwest. Cass Lake was a double pleasure. Pretty girls sunbathed on the public beach and large splake (brook trout x lake trout hybrid) roamed the drop-offs. I had better luck with the splake. Elizabeth Lake had rainbows as well. Pontiac Lake and Watkins Lake gave me some great largemouth bass on poppers. All of these lakes are in Oakland county and continue to provide excellent fly-fishing. A bit northwest at the Oakland/Livingston county line, Kensington State Park features Kent Lake for bluegills and bass.

The Clinton River runs in a south easterly direction from the Pontiac area through the Rochester-Utica Recreation Area, Mt. Clemens, and into Lake St. Clair. It supports a sizable run of steelhead. A bit further north, Paint Creek originates at Lake Orion and flows southeast through the town of Rochester. Thanks to the concerted efforts of many conservation groups and the cooperation of private land owners, Paint Creek has been revitalized. It now supports a healthy brown trout population and provides pleasurable fly-angling to many. This is a small, delicate, demanding stream, but very worthwhile. South Branch Supply on University in Rochester will provide reliable information on current conditions.

CHRIS VINCENT

John Vincent holds a typical Lake St. Clair smallmouth.

*TV producer Jerry Kunnath works the camera
for a Lake St. Clair episode with Chris Vincent and the author.*

A short drive west of Detroit on I-94, Ann Arbor is bisected by the Huron River. This is a true "blue ribbon" smallmouth bass stream. The Huron's best bass fishing is usually in the morning and evening. Fly-rodders typically use streamers, Woolly Buggers, poppers, sliders, and crayfish patterns. The best reach is from the small town of Dexter through Ann Arbor. The river's flow is interrupted by dams and ponds and these ponds or backwaters also produce excellent fly-fishing. During late July and August the Huron has a spectacular hatch of *Ephoron leukon*—the White Fly. This mayfly hatches and matures sexually the same evening, so you can expect to change patterns quickly if the bass are finicky on a particular day. Normally, a White Wulff in size 12 will fool all the fish you care to handle. But, there are days when the bigger bass are extremely critical. Carry some emerger, Compara-dun, and spinner patterns just in case. MacGregor's Outdoors is a full-line, full-service fly-shop staffed with serious anglers. The shop is on North Main Street in Ann Arbor. They have up-to-the-minute information and all the right patterns for the Huron. They will also tell you "where" on the river. The best angling locations vary throughout the season and, although access is pretty good throughout, it's best to zero-in on the stretches where the big smallmouth are most active.

Lake St. Clair

One word describes the fly-rod action with smallmouth bass on lake St. Clair—fabulous!

This is a "connector" lake, a body of water between the St. Clair and Detroit rivers. The St. Clair River is the outlet for the upper Great Lakes. It starts at Port Huron and enters (creates) Lake St. Clair at Algonac. The Detroit River is the outlet of Lake St. Clair and is the major inflow for the lower Great Lakes. It begins at the narrow southwest corner of the lake between Detroit and Windsor.

Lake St. Clair is probably the best angling lake in an urban area on the planet. It has a surface area of 420 square miles. Its maximum depth is 25 feet and the average depth is a little over 13 feet. The Great Lakes shipping navigation channel is 32 feet deep and 18 miles long as it bisects the lake.

On the Michigan side of Lake St. Clair, the shoreline is heavily developed from Algonac all the way to Grosse Pointe and Detroit. The Canadian side is more open and mostly "wild" with channels, protected bays, and extensive wetlands.

The lake supports a wide variety of fish, but the species of most interest to fly-anglers are smallmouth bass, largemouth bass, carp, northern pike, and musky. Armed with two outfits and a variety of flies, a fly-angler can pursue all five on a single outing. An 8 weight outfit is about right for bass and carp, but take along a 10-weight for the large northerns and the possibility of a world-record musky. Your rods should have some real backbone both for casting in the ever-present wind and for fighting very large fish. Many of the lake's bass top five pounds (both largemouth and smallmouth) the northerns often exceed 20 pounds, and there are muskys in Lake St. Clair that grow well beyond 50 pounds.

This a fertile body of water. Its bottom is largely silt and sand with some gravel and rock. There are extensive weed beds both in the lake proper and throughout the bays and channels. Cattails and bulrushes are common and provide natural cover across the extensive flats. Excepting periods of high wind, the water is clear and sight-fishing the shallow flats is superb. Both species of bass, northerns, muskys, and carp can be seen ghosting across the sand or suspending motionless in ambush close to the cattails, bulrushes and high grass islands.

How do you fish it? Where do you start? Well, since we're dealing with a surface area of over 400 square miles, a lot of the general wisdom we might apply to a pond or small lake of just a few acres goes right out the window. It is shallow and open for many miles and any moderate wind can make the lake unsafe for the inexperienced angler in a small craft. And, it is split into both USA (Michigan) and Canadian (Ontario) jurisdiction with the added spice of Indian Reservation water, so you need to know where you are going to fish and have the appropriate licenses. Despite the nearly 20 public and private launching facilities, the numerous bays, inlets, flats, islands, and points, this is an imposing, daunting piece of water to explore on your own.

My recommendation is to hire a guide. There are guides on both Canadian and U.S. shores that specialize in everything from perch to musky. Nearly every baitshop, tackle shop, and marina (and those are numerous) can refer you to a guide that knows the water, but very few are versed in fly-fishing requirements.

To my knowledge, there is only one strictly fly-fishing guide service on Lake St. Clair and that is the operation run by the Flymart Flyshops of Royal Oak and St. Clair Shores on the Michigan side. The Flymart stores are run by brothers John and Chris Vincent, two highly regarded anglers and conservationists. Their guide service covers all of the metro area lakes, but for this book (and my own obsession) I wanted to fish Lake St. Clair from their 18-foot Scout flats boat. One of Chris' clients had recently caught and released a 45-pound (estimated) female musky. This and the knowledge that we'd fish shallow, clear water for large bass charged me with anticipation.

Chris was waiting for me when I walked out of the hotel at 6 a.m. on a very cool mid-July morning. The trailered flats skiff, complete with poling platform, made me think of the Florida Keys, but the cold wind brought me back to Michigan in a hurry. We stopped and bought cups of "fogbuster" coffee and drove north on Interstate 94 to Metropolitan Parkway, then east about four miles to Metropolitan Park and the public boat launch where we met Jerry and Steve Kunnath of Vermillion Productions and their friend, Bob Doster. Vermillion Productions and Flymart are producing a television series on fly-fishing and bird hunting for the Outdoor Channel called "Fly Rod & Gun Outdoors." Their intent was

A careful release of a hefty bass.

Working poppers near the grass edges at dawn.

This largemouth ate a black Woolly Bugger, then buried itself in the weeds.

to video tape the day on Lake St. Clair for a show to air during 2002.

The flats boat was in the water, engine at idle and the camera crew boat was being launched when the wind strengthened. This was mid-summer. Chris and I were wearing tropical-weight clothing and we began to shiver. We could see white caps beyond the breakwater and watched two flights of ducks bank and settle into the sheltered waters of the boat-launch area. "Do you have an extra windbreaker or rain parka?" I asked

Chris. He did, thankfully. We secured the fly-rods and other gear, drained our coffee, and headed out on to the big lake.

Our initial run was several miles at speed to some cattail and bulrush islands in Big Muscamoot Bay. Chris' hope was to find shelter from the wind and clear water on the lee sides of the islands. Hopefully, we would be able to see the big fish (pike and musky) and cast large streamers, or drop deer-hair bugs tight to the vegetation for bass.

Chris handed me an 8-weight, 9-foot set-up with a weight-forward floating line, heavy leader, and a handsome, big-eyed, deer-hair frog. "Drop the frog next to the bulrushes, let it sit for a few seconds, then 'pop it' and retrieve slowly with a series of pops." This was easier said than done. The wind was fierce and Chris was unable to hold the boat from the poling platform. And, of course, my casting was less than perfect. He engaged the powerful electric trolling motor to fight the wind-enforced, high-speed drift and we struggled along the edges of several grass humps hoping to find an aggressive smallmouth. No luck.

The wind chill factor is something we're accustomed to in Michigan, but not in July. "This is incredible! Look at the ducks. This is more like October!" Chris said. I turned and watched a small group of bluebills bob and weave low over the white caps. "Let's run to the big islands and fish the sheltered channels," he added. There was no argument from me.

We ran into Fisher Bay and from there entered a series of narrow, protected channels that cut through sections of Dickinson Island. These channels are rich in

This magnificent female musky was caught and posed for just one photograph before being carefully released. She ate a large Deceiver cast from Chris Vincent's flats boat on Lake St. Clair.

had told me to drop it. I stripped the bug out from under the bridge and popped it once. From directly below, a shadow appeared, angled upward, and a huge mouth sucked the fly down. The fish turned and I practiced my "tarpon" strike. Weight and power surged through the rod and the heavy bass fought to gain cover. Jerry Kunnath was on the video camera at the time. He yelled, "I got it. I got the strike perfectly." After a few powerful surges, Chris "lipped" the bass for a few quick photos and released it unharmed. We didn't tape or weight it, but it was one of the biggest largemouth I had caught on a fly.

It was hard to imagine, but the wind actually began to blow harder. My hands and face were turning blue. Chris and the TV production crew didn't look much better. "Let's make a drift along the Middle Channel (between Dickinson Island and Harsen's Island) for big pike and musky," Chris suggested. Just the thought of a musky warmed me and we moved to the wide, deep channel.

Chris handed me a 10-weight rod with a 250-grain sinker, a short leader with heavy shock tippet and a seven-inch chartreuse streamer that looked much like the giant patterns one might throw in Maine's tidal pools for striped bass. Chris set the boat so the wind would blow us down the channel and he used the electric motor and depth finder to hold us in the proper position.

About half way down the channel I felt a heavy thud on the fly, then a heavier pull, then nothing. We checked the rig and the fly was gone. What chomps through a 60-pound shock tippet? In my heart, I knew. I envisioned a huge musky's baleful stare. Chris retied the leader, selected a new fly and said, "Break's over, back to work." We had drifted another 100 yards or so when another fish struck. This was a much lighter feeling and after a couple of minutes we boated a northern pike of about 25 inches. It was time to call it a day. The film crew had some decent footage and we were practically frozen. It's a tribute to Chris' guiding skill and knowledge of the lake that we were able to catch anything under such adverse weather conditions.

We made the run back to the launch area at Metropark in short order and lunged for the extra thermos of coffee in the back seat of the truck.

Lake St. Clair more often than not gives up 20-40 smallmouth per day to a moderately skilled fly-angler. These bass are big, often in excess of four pounds. Add in a few largemouth, northerns, and the chance at a world-record musky in a wilderness, big-water setting in the shadow of Detroit's skyline, and you have the best urban fly-fishing in the world.

vegetation and forage for game fish. Best of all, the wind did not freeze or beat us silly. I changed colors on the deer-hair popping bug and began to throw short casts to small openings in the weeds. Chris pointed to a cardtable-sized clear spot and I dropped the bug pretty near its center. But, I dropped the line from my left hand, then stepped on the loose line on the casting platform. Perfect. Just as I bent (and took my eyes off the bug) to free the line, a large bass exploded on the bug. "Hit him," Chris ordered. I tried, but all I had was slack. The fish was gone. "Timing is everything," he added. I agreed. The bass's timing was perfect—dead, solid perfect.

Chris moved our boat to within about 40 feet of a road bridge over the channel. "We moved a really nice bass right here yesterday, but couldn't hook it. Drop the bug tight to the concrete piling on the left side—a little bit under the bridge—then pop it back to us." I took a deep breath, checked the coils of line and made the cast. Fortune smiled. The fly went exactly where Chris

Lansing Area

ANDY BUSH

Above: Steve Swihart silhouettes a nice Grand River smallmouth at dawn.

Right: Kelly Neuman with a typical smallmouth.

Lansing is the state capital. That, the presence of the main campus of Michigan State University in East Lansing, and the headquarters of the (soon-to-be-phased-out) Oldsmobile Division of General Motors builds a substantial population base in the metropolitan area. About 300,000 is a reasonable guess. In addition to the Grand River covered here, fly-anglers should look at Lake Ovid in Sleepy Hollow State Park north of East Lansing. This lovely park has 181 campsites and a public boat launch. Lake Ovid has two large islands and a long, irregular shoreline with extensive points, bays and coves. A bit south and right off Marsh Road in Haslett you will find Lake Lansing. This lake sits just a few minutes off the I-69 expressway to the east of the city complex. It has surprisingly good fly-fishing for largemouth bass and northern pike. Not to be ignored

is the possibility of hooking a tiger musky—Lake Lansing has them in good numbers. M. Chance Fly Fishing Specialties in nearby Okemos will give you accurate information on current conditions. They will probably recommend a 9-foot, 8-weight outfit and some Deceivers, Woolly Buggers, and deer-hair popping bugs as a starting point.

Grand River

A nice bass caught in urban Lansing.

This river has the longest flow of all rivers in the state of Michigan. It begins at the Lake Le Ann, Mirror Lake, Grand Lake chain at the border of Jackson and Hillsdale counties south of the city of Jackson in southern Michigan. Its flow from the headwaters is northward through Jackson to near the border of Jackson and Ingham counties where it bends westward, then northwest and north through Lansing. After looping through Lansing, the Grand runs westward into Ionia County, then north through Portland, then westward again through Grand Rapids and on to Grand Haven and the mouth at Lake Michigan.

Throughout this course of over 240 miles, the Grand supports a diverse fishery for the fly-angler willing to explore big, flowing water. Northern pike, carp, smallmouth bass, steelhead, and salmon are the primary targets. Many of the Grand's numerous tributaries, like the Looking Glass and Red Cedar near Lansing and the Rogue (see separate coverage) near Grand Rapids, provide exceptional fly-fishing as well.

The Looking Glass and Red Cedar enter the Grand in the Lansing area. The Red Cedar winds through the beautiful campus of Michigan State University.

Alumnus and local fly-fishing expert, Andy Bush confessed to me that he spent a lot of free time (and time that perhaps should have spent in the MSU library) fly-fishing for smallmouth bass in the Red Cedar. "I learned to fly-fish there. I love it," he said.

The Grand River in the Lansing area should be considered in three parts, the upper stretch from Jackson to the Lansing city limits, the middle reach within the city of Lansing, and the lower run from the west edge of Lansing to the city of Portland.

The upper stretch has a very slow flow. Its meandering slide from Jackson to Lansing supports northern pike, walleyes, and smallmouth bass. Generally speaking, these predators will be found in close proximity to brush cover. Local fly-angler, Steve Swihart likes bright-colored streamers and foam surface poppers for the northerns. These are not large fish, but are a lot of fun on a medium-weight fly-rod. Steve and Andy use smaller leech patterns, particularly a size 6 purple Strip Leech, for the walleyes.

Two of the better access points for the upper stretch are at Bunker Highway and Columbia Road. Both of these spots have roadside parks that provide space to leave a vehicle and get into the river. It should be noted that the upper stretch is difficult to wade in many areas. It has a mix of deep water and slow pools with a soft bottom, but the Natural Area off Grovenburg Road and the area upstream from the Waverly Road bridge have hard-bottom runs. Both of these areas have solid smallmouth bass populations as well as northerns and walleye. The middle reach of the river, from Dimondale through the city of Lansing is, for the most part, difficult to fish for the fly-angler. Several dams check the flow and the dam at Moores Park stops the steelhead and salmon runs from reaching further upstream. The North Lansing dam and the Brinke fish ladder are checkpoints to monitor fish migrations. The Red Cedar enters the Grand just upstream from the fish ladder and is much better suited to fly-fishing. Over the years, Andy has caught and released 40-inch pike, 20-inch smallmouth, 10-pound coho salmon, and 15-pound steelhead in the lower Red Cedar. Best access points for the Red Cedar are the county parks at Okemos, Vanalta, and Meridian roads.

The lower run, from Lansing to Portland, is the real gem of the system for fly-angling. The water is easy to wade and loaded with aggressive bass. Boulders are the main fish-holding feature in this section and one mid-river rock may shelter a half dozen fish willing to smack your streamer or popper.

In mid-summer, weed lines develop and the fish move to the edges of the weeds to ambush prey. An adult damselfly pattern drifting over the weed lines will usually produce aggressive strikes. Day in and day out, streamers are the first choice for consistency. Carry Clouser Minnows, Zoo Cougars, leech patterns, Woolly Buggers, and a few foam-bodied poppers. Poppers in white, green, or yellow, tied with a marabou tail on size 8 hooks produce throughout the summer.

In addition to the heavy-bodied smallmouth, this section of the river supports a fishable population of solid, spooky carp. This is mostly sight-fishing on knee-deep flats. It is a hunting—stalking game that requires a very careful delivery in smooth, shallow water. Carp on the flats are ultra-selective and difficult to approach. A sloppy cast or a shadow will spook them. Andy and Steve like nymph patterns with the built-in action of marabou and philoplume feathers. Andy Bush's favorite is a Philoplume Hex Nymph complete with burned mono eyes. Small realistic patterns and fluorocarbon tippet give the angler a distinct advantage.

The water near Grant Woods Park and Delta Mills has a mix of flats and weed-cover runs with good populations of both smallmouth and carp. The run downstream from Delta Mills is a good place to fish

Red horse suckers take flies fished near the bottom. Scott Smith caught this record fish on a crayfish pattern.

ANDY BUSH

Andy Bush catches large carp with careful casting and small nymph patterns.

cone-head Woolly Buggers in black and olive. The water below Grand Ledge dam at Fitzgerald Park has a series of long gravel flats that attract salmon in the fall. Lincoln Brick Park is across the river from Fitzgerald Park. It is a great place to set up for an evening. The park features a lengthy nature trail that follows the river and makes it possible to fish downstream for a considerable period of time with only a five-minute walk back up the trail to your vehicle. This area has a deep center run with boulders that holds most of the fish. A white streamer cast to the rocks and boulders is effective most of the time for smallmouth.

The Portland State Game Area provides access to a lot of good water. The river widens here and presents easy wading and high sport with both smallmouth bass and carp. In October the gravel bars often fill with coho salmon if the water conditions are right—meaning adequate rainfall to raise the level of the river. As the Grand flows into the town of Portland it merges with the Looking Glass. This is a fine fishery for anglers who like smaller water. The smallmouth are large and numerous and there is a favorable mix of gravel and rock to shelter them.

There are more fly-angling opportunities as the Grand widens, deepens and heads to Grand Rapids and on to Lake Michigan. Check with local fly-shops (see appendix) for opportunities in the main river and tributaries in the Grand Rapids area. For the Lansing area, check in with the folks at M. Chance Fly Fishing Specialties in Okemos.

Colorful steelhead and salmon flies used near Lansing.

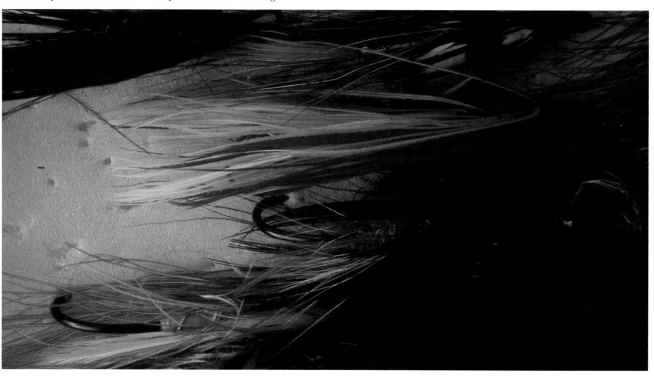

Grand Rapids Area

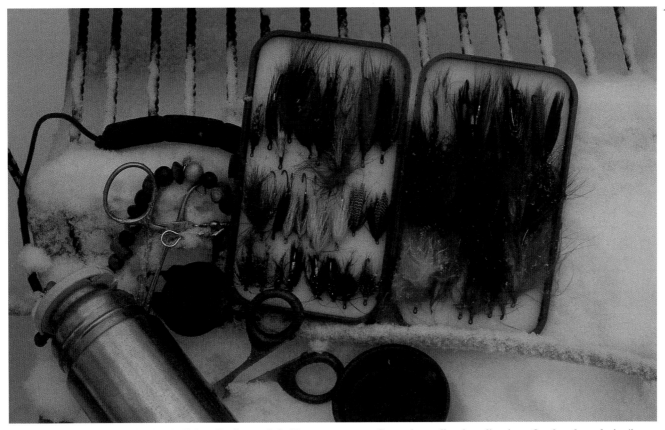

Grand Rapids is in Michigan's "lake-effect" snow belt. Heavy snows can flavor the steelhead angling from October through April.

The Grand Rapids metropolitan area is second only to Detroit and its suburbs in terms of population density in the state of Michigan. The greater Grand Rapids metropolitan base is in southwestern Kent County and southeastern Ottawa County. The city proper is bisected by the westward flowing Grand River which is fed by the Flat River at the town of Lowell to the east and by the Rogue which joins the Grand to the north of the city. Many of the area's resident and visiting fly-anglers head north to the Pere Marquette, Muskegon, and Manistee rivers, or the lakes and ponds near Cadillac and Traverse City for trout, steelhead, salmon, bass, and northern pike. Just "going fishing," getting in the car and making a trip, is part of the fun, but, the fact is, truly excellent fly-angling opportunities are available much closer to home.

In addition to the Rogue and Flat rivers and Long Lake featured here, the Grand Rapids area presents other fly-fishing venues worth exploring. The popular steelhead fishery of the Grand River, right in the city, is more suited to bait-angling than fly-fishing, but

fly-anglers do take fish there. Considerable care must be exercised while wading; each year it seems that at least one incautious sole is drowned while steelhead angling "downtown."

To the city's south and slightly east, Gun Lake sits at the border of Allegan and Barry counties. This is a large lake with prominent points and bays. It features public boat launches on the west and north sides and is bordered by Yankee Springs State Recreational Area and Yankee Springs State Park on the north and east sides. It has good fishing for both largemouth and smallmouth bass.

Lincoln Lake is near the corner of Kent and Montcalm counties about 40 minutes northeast of Grand Rapids. This stream-freshened lake has very good fly-fishing in the spring and fall for tiger musky, northern pike, and largemouth bass. Due south from Lincoln Lake and due east from Grand Rapids you will find Murray Lake near the Kent and Ionia county line. Murray Lake features a large, bisecting peninsula and harbors tiger musky, northern pike and bass.

The Rogue River

This small stream begins at the junction of several small creeks in the Rogue River State Game Area just a few miles north of Grand Rapids. It flows southward past the town of Sparta, then loops east and north before turning south again at Rockford. It continues southward from Rockford to its confluence with the Grand.

Throughout its short course, the Rogue is noted as a fine trout stream. Both brown and rainbow trout are present from the mouth at West River Road to the headwaters in the state game area. Some of these fish reach significant size and trout of 15-plus inches are regularly taken during the Rogue's prolific hatches as well as on attractor nymphs and streamers. All of the major mayfly hatches in west Michigan appear on the Rogue, but special consideration should be given to the whitefly emergence and spinner fall of August and early September. Hendricksons, Sulphurs, various olives, caddis, and stoneflies also bring good fish to the surface during their specific time slots. The trout can be pretty demanding; they require a good pattern carefully cast and presented drag-free. Remember, this stream is within 30 minutes of nearly 600,000 people!

Within the city limits of the handsome village of Rockford, a small dam halts the upstream migration of salmon, steelhead, and Lake Michigan-dwelling brown trout. From this dam downsteam to the Grand River, the attention turns from resident stream trout to migratory salmonids from September through April. The salmon (king or chinook) make their first appearance in late August with growing numbers through September and early October. They reach weights approaching 30 pounds and are an impressive sight as they fan gravel and push submarine-like wakes through the shallow riffles of this small river. Fall steelhead follow the salmon and maintain fishable numbers throughout winter and into spring when the "fall" run is joined by waves of fresh fish in from Lake Michigan. The steelhead in the Rogue are excellent fly-rod trophies. They are aggressive and healthy; some fish reach lengths over 34 inches and a few are caught and released each year that approach 40 inches. These huge steelhead are lifetime milestones for a fly-angler. Landing a running, leaping silver rampage in a 50-foot-wide shallow stream is high anxiety and problematic, intense exercise.

Glen Blackwood nymphing for fall steelhead on the Rogue River.

This is a favorite run of Glen's a bit downstream from Sowerby Park.

The large brown trout up from Lake Michigan follow the salmon to the same gravel redds at roughly the same time. Although the browns spawn a bit later than the salmon, they seem happy enough to gorge (along with fall steelhead) on the eggs and dislodged nymphs pushed into the flow by the furious activity of the chinook. The fall brown-trout run is made up of fish from about 22 to 27 inches. These are meritorious and desirable in their own right—a 6- or 7-pound brown trout is a dream fish for most fly-anglers. The Rogue has plenty of easy, public-access points. Within Rockford's city limits (below the dam), an excellent starting point is at Richardsons Sowerby Park. This is a long and narrow city-owned strip of land on the west side of the stream. The total acreage is a bit over 4.5, which doesn't sound like much but is enough to provide access to some excellent gravel areas, riffles and holding pools.

The last time I visited the Rogue, I was guided by local expert, Glen Blackwood. Glen is the proprietor of The Great Lakes Fly Fishing Company, a complete, pro fly-shop on 10 Mile Road in Rockford. He took me to the Richardsons Sowerby Park water in the soft morning light of early October. We saw salmon holding in the pools and deeper pockets and a few stirring gravel near the banks. Smaller, lighter forms ghosted up to the downstream edge of several salmon redds before turning and sliding back to deeper, darker water. We guessed them to be brown trout. One ethereal wisp of about 30 inches flashed through a shallow run and simply evaporated like dispersing smoke. I thought it to be a steelhead.

Glen showed me his favorite nymphing rig for this shallow reach. He used a 9.5-foot, 7-weight rod with a floating line and a leader of about 10 feet tapered to an 8-pound-test tippet. He positioned a strike indicator at a point on the leader that would approximate twice the depth of the water. Since the indicator could be easily moved up and down the leader, adjustments to different depths took just seconds. He fished a small Hare's Ear Nymph as a dropper and a black, Egg Sucking Leech as the point fly. A very small split shot was sufficient to put the flies at the proper depth but did not interfere with his fly-casting.

The soft morning turned to bright sunlight too quickly and the fish moved to the deepest water available to sulk. The river was much lower than normal for the time of year and incredibly clear due to an extended drought. Happily, a few minutes before we had to leave, Glen's indicator jerked forward and he connected with a large, fresh hen salmon. Briefly, the fish ran upstream, thrashed, jumped and broke off. I was busy burning film in hopes of a good photograph of the fish on the surface, or better yet, in the air. On the way back to his fly-shop Glen made some general tackle suggestions for the Rogue. He recommends a 9.5-foot rod for a 7- or 8-weight line as a good choice for salmon, steelhead and fall browns. "Lighter rods—say 5- and 6- weights are just too light in the hands of most anglers," he said. Glen uses high-quality, disk-drag reels with ample backing (100 yards or so). He feels the fly assortment can be kept relatively simple. "A few egg flies in various colors, Egg Sucking Leeches, Hare's Ears, Pheasant Tails, caddis, and stonefly nymphs will cover the bases." For general fly-fishing for stream trout, a 9-foot, 4- or 5-weight rod is right most of the time. Fly selection depends, of course, on the time of year and prevailing insect activity.

Flat River

This river is a smallmouth bass dream stream. It is lightly fished with miles of easily accessible and productive bass water in a scenic rural setting. Some of the Flat's best fishing and more beautiful vistas are within 20 minutes of the Grand Rapids city center.

The Flat forms in northern Montcalm County in the Six Lakes area just west of the town of Edmore. From there it flows southerly and a bit west through Greenville, crosses into Ionia County and through Belding, then meanders through a series of wide curves to the southwest and joins the Grand at the town of Lowell in extreme western Kent County.

The Flat River at Fallasburg Park teems with aggressive smallmouth bass.

The best smallmouth fishing, in terms of size and numbers of fish and consistency of action, is from Greenville to the mouth. In this reach the river ranges in width from about 100 to 150 feet. Its depth varies from ankle to nose deep (and more!) and wading is reasonably easy. The bottom is mixed clay, sand, gravel, and large rocks. The Flat builds a base of heavy weeds and grass in the late summer and bass often use the channels between beds of grass as ambush points. The Flat has a classic, slow-moving pool-rapid-riffle configuration with small islands, undercut banks, deep pockets, and visible seams (quick depth changes) that provide cover for the aggressive smallmouth.

The river also features abundant aquatic life. All the major mayfly hatches, including *Hexagenia limbata*, are present and will bring bass to the surface during both emergence periods and spinner falls. Dace, chubs, shiners, crayfish, stoneflies, and caddis round out the menu. Bob Braendle and Glen Blackwood of the Great Lakes Fly Fishing Company told me that the best hatches are the brown drakes, the *Hex*, and the *Ephoron* (white fly).

One of the best and certainly one of the most scenic places to try the Flat River is at Fallasburg Park just a short drive north of Lowell. This beautiful park has 1 1/2 miles of river frontage in a setting of mixed hardwoods and rolling hills. Not the least of its alluring features is a restored, wooden, covered bridge over the river in a location that, happily, also provides very good fly-fishing. Fishing through the park is a blend of wild excitement and gentile accommodation. The pugnacious bass provide the excitement and the gentle but stunning scenery mixed with parking, picnic, and rest room facilities do the rest.

Glen Blackwood's fly-shop offers guide service on the Flat. They recommend 9-foot, 7- or 8-weight rods, dry-fly patterns to match the hatch, a selection of deer-hair, top-water poppers and sliders, and streamers including Shenk's White Fly, Clouser Minnows, yellow Muddlers, and Near'nuff Sculpins.

In addition to smallmouth bass, fly-anglers will also likely encounter northern pike and carp. The northerns will eat the same streamers, poppers, and sliders as the bass. The carp are best pursued with nymphs and small crayfish patters.

A quick look at county maps indicate the presence of several small dams with backwater ponds. Although I have not fished them, Glen informed me that the fly-angling can be excellent in these ponds. They receive very little pressure in general and the fish rarely see an artificial fly of any kind.

Hexagenia limbata dun.

Long Lake

This small lake of about 47 acres sits near the northwest corner of Kent County about 30 minutes north of Grand Rapids and 20 minutes northwest of Rockford just south of MI Hwy. 46 (17 Mile Road) and west of I-131.

Long Lake sits in a quiet, rural nest surrounded by mixed agriculture lands and wild hardwoods. Long Lake Park provides easy access to the water along with the expected facilities—parking, picnic tables, children's play areas, and rest rooms. Motors are not allowed on this body of water and this is a significant plus in my opinion. No roaring ski boats or personal watercraft interrupt a peaceful float in canoe or tube.

The lake's bottom is a mix of sand and silt. It has weedy edges, moderate depth, and abundant forage. Long Lake supports northern pike, largemouth bass and panfish with good size and in sufficient numbers to produce a memorable day on the water.

A selection of bass and pike-sized poppers and sliders, a few Clouser Minnows, a crayfish pattern or two, and a handful of panfish patterns like rubber-legged crickets, small poppers, and a few

A "banded" swan and mate cruise the shoreline of Long Lake.
Top: Beautiful and serene, Long Lake is lightly fished.

nymphs such as Hare's Ears and black or yellow Woolly Worms are about all you'll need for flies. If panfish are your target, a 9-foot, 4- or 5-weight is ideal. Bass and pike require a heftier set-up; you could connect to a very large northern. I'd pick a 9-foot, 8-weight with a floating line and an extra spool for the reel with a sink-tip for throwing the bigger bugs for pike and bass.

II
West Coast Region

This is Michigan's Gold Coast. It is one incredibly long and beautiful beach from the state line with Indiana to the Straits of Mackinac at McGulpin Point at the northern extreme of the Lower Peninsula. A simple listing of the streams, creeks, rivers, lakes, and ponds—names only—would make a bigger volume than my local phone directory.

So much water, so little time. Selection is difficult. The St. Joe, a fantastic steelhead fishery, is not included here. Neither are the Kalamazoo, White, Pentwater, Big Sable, Little Manistee, Betsie, Platte, Boardman, and Jordan rivers. They are all covered in detail in other publications. The lakes and ponds not included, along with lesser-known streams, would make up the phone book referred to above.

A fly-angler really can't go wrong on the west side of Michigan. Bass, northerns, muskys, panfish, carp, trout, and salmon waters—still and moving—are everywhere. I seriously doubt if there is a point on the map that is more than 15 minutes from good fly-fishing.

What follows here is some of the best. They are waters that will please you: More importantly, they are points of departure for your own exploration.

Muskegon River

This beautiful chrome steelhead is typical of late-winter-run fish in the Muskegon.

The stretch of the Muskegon that is most widely regarded as "Blue-Ribbon" fly-fishing water is the run of approximately 21 miles from Croton Dam in Newaygo County to Bridgeton. This is mostly trout, steelhead, and salmon water and 99 percent of the attention is centered on these species. The trout fishing can be exceptional and when the Muskegon is "hot," the angling will rival that found on the best rivers in North America. This big river often combines the attributes and charms of other rivers and I have heard it described as a very large version or Pennsylvania's Letort, or Idaho's Silver Creek.

Although most of the angling pressure is centered below Croton Dam, the Muskegon fishes well throughout its course from Houghton Lake to Lake Michigan. The upper reaches are primarily small-mouth bass, walleye, and northern pike habitat. Coldwater feeder streams support trout and many drop down into the larger river. Large browns, and less frequently rainbows, are caught sporadically through-out the year by fly-fishers in search of smallmouth bass. And the backwater ponds behind the dams, specif-ically Croton Pond and Hardy Reservoir, have strong smallmouth populations and dense mayfly hatches (*Ephoron leukon*—White Fly and *Hexagenia limbata*—giant Michigan mayfly) that bring bass to the surface in crashing, twilight feeding lunges.

Still, with all the upriver riches, the best fly-angling is below Croton. A perfectly reasonable scenario in the spring or fall would include, but not be limited to, the following: The angler starts with a 3-weight rod, long and fine leader, and midge patterns. Casting to visibly feeding browns and rainbows at the edges, seams, and in the expansive pools, the angler will take chunky trout from 12 to 16-plus inches in length. If caddis or mayfly activity occurs, a switch to a 4- or 5-weight will handle fish to the 20-inch range. A two-handed Spey rod will be used to deliver and swing undulating marabou patterns like the Tequila Sunrise through the gravel runs and pockets for steelhead. If this scenario takes place in September, the gravel will hold Alaska-sized salmon and the darker water below will harbor steelhead. Lastly, a 9-foot, 7-weight rod, full-sinking line and stout, short leader will be employed to pulse large streamers for Seeforellen brown trout in the 10-plus-pound range. All of this can take place in 200 yards of river!

The Federal Energy Relicensing Committee (FERC) has mandated "run of the river" flows for the Muskegon (and other rivers). Since the implementation of this decree, natural reproduction for stream trout, salmon, steelhead, and Seeforellen brown trout has increased dramatically. Current estimates suggest that the ratio of wild to stocked steelhead has soared to

MATT SUPINSKI

Resident rainbows grow large on the Muskegon's prolific hatches.

60% wild fish and that approximately 3,000,000 king salmon smolts are born in the river annually.

All of this bounty attracts people. There is a lot of angling pressure on the Muskegon, probably the highest number of angler hours per season in Michigan. And the heaviest concentration of pressure comes during the fall salmon madness and the spring steelhead run. During these two periods I suggest you pick your days

Waving aquatic grasses
nourish and shelter the Muskegon's insects.

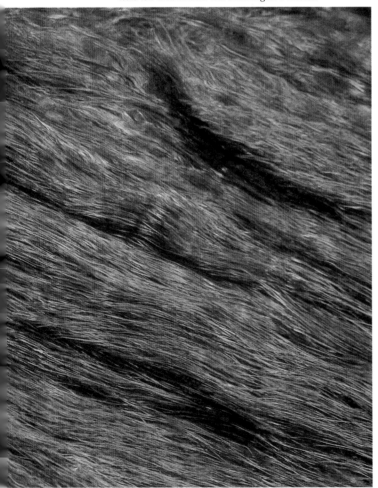

carefully. Avoid weekends if at all possible. Certainly mid-week is the best choice. During the "run," weekends on the Muskegon start on Friday mornings and end late afternoon on Mondays.

Although this is large water by any standard and guided float trips provide a distinct advantage, there is plenty of walk-in access for the wading angler. The San Juan Flats and Pine Street (Kimball Park) are two favorites in the upper stretch. Despite considerable pressure, the angling can be superb all year long. There are prolific hatches here—midges, mayflies, and caddis. The bottom shelters abundant populations of crayfish and sculpins along with juvenile steelhead and salmon. Brown and rainbow trout here are fat and happy but not stupid. Careful presentation and a precise match of the dominant bug are absolutely necessary. There are additional walk-in accesses at the A-Frame High Banks (along 72nd St.), Henning Park, Newaygo Park, and more.

My two most recent adventures on the Muskegon evoke images in stark contrast. In mid-February the long driveway leading to the Gray Drake Lodge was packed hard with snow. Three deer, standing at the edge of my vision, seemed to be knee deep. Only their steamy breath gave them away in the twilight. The radio weather witch cackled, "It's 10 degrees out there. Tomorrow will be clear and cold." At the foot of the steep hill below the lodge, the Muskegon curled black and mysterious.

Matt and Laurie Supinski own the Gray Drake which provides trophy fishing (catch and release only) guide services and first-class accommodations for visiting fly-anglers. Matt threatened me with his Joe Cocker and Rod Stewart imitations should I even mention the cold. Having suffered that torture the previous St. Patrick's Day, I clammed up. "We'll do fine. The water is cold but warms enough to activate the fish by 10 a.m. There are quite a few steelhead in the deep pools. We'll fish eggs and nymphs," he said. "Maggie Taylor is here from Los Angeles; she'll join us tomorrow." I was up early, shuffling through the lodge to the kitchen and its life-saving coffee maker. Maggie was already there and the pot was brewing. A good beginning. We both noticed a male voice singing. It was Matt of course. The song was "Unchain My Heart," a good one, I thought, for a winter's steelhead serenade.

The air temperature was 18 degrees F. and the water tested at 35 when Matt pushed the boat into the current. As the sun rose further in the southeastern sky, the day warmed slightly. Maggie had an all-too-brief hook-up with a big steelhead that ran straight toward us as she tried vainly to set the hook. I caught a fat brown trout on a Hare's Ear Nymph. The fish was about 15 inches and put on a vigorous, active defense considering the cold water.

Matt moved the boat a bit downstream and anchored in the sunlight (happily) at the very edge of a deeply shaded riffle that ran full and dark to the south bank. Maggie muttered from deep in her fleece wrap, "I'm a frozen Southern California girl! You cast." I did. On the third or fourth drift, the egg pattern stopped and I raised the rod. A magnificent silver hen rushed to the surface, thrashed and rolled, then showed us her good stuff. If was over in just a few short minutes. She lay in the big net while I removed the hook and Matt snapped several photos. Her energy returned quickly and she shot out from the soft water and into the current with power. I thought aloud that "this is about the most fun a simple country boy can have in February." Smiles all around.

We moved with the current, drifting slowly in the warmth of the pale winter sunlight. Our collective mood was content as we approached the Gray Drake's "home pool." Matt explained that several large steelhead had been holding in the deep water and that the fishing had been as good here as anywhere else on the river for the past several days. The added bonus was clear; his dock, the uphill path, and lodge were thirty yards away. Maggie was enjoying the modest sunshine and I was loading a fresh roll of film into my camera. She and I agreed that Matt should make a few casts and he complied. His first and only cast produced a fish—not just any fish—an incredible 35-inch buck. The big male fought deep, hard, and long. I netted him for Matt and we all marveled at the thick, powerful body and developing kype. We called the game complete when the big steelhead stroked out and away from Matt's grip.

Andy Bush drifts nymphs below a salmon redd hoping for a hungry fall steelhead.

Fall on the Muskegon River.

Early October sets another stage with different players. Thousands of Pacific salmon push wakes across shallow gravel bars and cruise through the clear pools with obvious purpose. The aquatic vegetation is lush, the sun is warm, and the banks are on fire with the wild fluorescence of sumac, sugar and red maple, crabapple, and aspen. Trout slide cautiously behind the spawning salmon and gobble drifting eggs or take station at the current edges to ambush insects and forage fish. Steelhead appear briefly as wisps of smoke then quickly evaporate into the darker runs and riffles.

Andy Bush, Steve Swihart and I launched Andy's boat on a warm, early October afternoon. We were amazed at the number of salmon; they were literally "wall to wall." Our intent was to fish streamers for trout, perhaps entice a steelhead to snatch a sculpin pattern or Woolly Bugger. Still, it was difficult to not be distracted by the thousands of giant salmon. They were everywhere—on the redds, splashing through the silt shallows near the banks, holding impatiently in deep pools, sliding over the waving field of verdant green aquatic grasses.

We stuck to our guns, or trout rods as the case happened to be. We caught several nice rainbows and browns in the 12-inch range on Buggers and Zoo Cougars, but did not make contact with a steelhead or big brown. It was all we could do to keep our streamers away from the big kings. A 30-pound, aggravated salmon and a 6-weight trout rod is a problematic connection.

The day was warm and sunny. The fall colors were brilliant. We caught fine trout and saw roughly 10,000 salmon on our short, lazy float. We shared "howdys"

The author carefully holds a Muskegon steelhead caught in February.

and small talk with others enjoying the day and soaked in the extravagant colors of a great Michigan river in the palm of autumn.

Most of the professional fly-shops in the area offer guide service on the Muskegon and there are some experienced, independent guides as well. The appendix lists some of the best. Before you visit, make a phone call or two to check on prevailing hatches and for the timing and strength of the steelhead run.

A typical Muskegon brown. This one ate a small caddis dry.

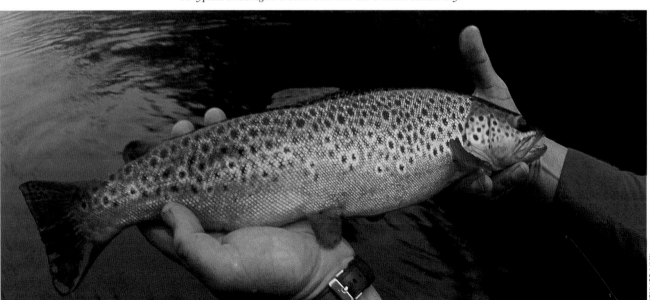

Pere Marquette

Angler extraordinaire Kelly Galloup runs a nymph through a PM run in late November.

Much of my early success in fly-fishing for steelhead and salmon centered on the "flies-only" water of the Pere Marquette. And within the fly-water, the upper section from M-37 to the Green Cottage was my favorite.

In the early 70s, Steve Nevala and I fished the runs of wallowing king salmon with little mid-week competition. If we saw a dozen other anglers during a day's outing we felt crowded. One of my most vivid memories of this era is a 40-minute battle with a 30-plus-pound male that swam several feet to slash and grab an orange-and-white marabou streamer. The big fish ran up and downstream several times and jumped with crashing abandon. We whooped and hollered and chased until Steve slid his large net under the fish. There was, of course, a lot of time before the net was needed and Steve used it to record my panic and the fish's thrashing runs on his eight millimeter movie camera. That really dates the episode. The fish hangs on my wall today, the largest salmon I have ever caught. And the movie film has been converted to VHS. Both bring back a wonderful slice of time.

Steelhead were then, and remain now, a much deeper passion. We didn't worry too much about what days to fish—as long as we had the spring run well bracketed. Even weekends were acceptable if that was when we could get free. The extravagant, nearly perfect spawning gravel runs pretty well through the entire length of the "flies-only" water, and steelhead use every yard of it. These are wild, born-in-the-river fish with great beauty, power, and a marked inclination to eat flies. Steelhead are trophies of such great desire that, even then, I would go through just about anything to get to the Pere Marquette. Many years ago I flew through an intense electrical storm to meet Steve at a western Michigan airport. The plane was hit by lightning and lost its interior lights (and I suspect more). The pilot announced that we were "safe" but would be a bit late. When we landed Steve remarked that I looked just a bit wane and ashen, then "Get your stuff. Let's go!"

Things are a little different now. The fish are still magnificent and still yearn for and rush the perfect spawning gravel in spring and fall, but so do many

*On another November day Kelly and I had the
Pere Marquette to ourselves.*

more anglers. You have to pick your times carefully to avoid crowding. To me, that is a vital component of angling pleasure.

The Pere Marquette is the most famous and popular steelhead river in the Great Lakes basin. It is inviting, easy to wade and fish, lovely with a capital L, and hosts strong runs of spring and fall/winter steelhead as well as very heavy runs of fall salmon. It is only two hours from Grand Rapids, two and one half hours from Kalamazoo, and five hours from Chicago. And, you should know that "weekends" during steelhead and salmon runs begin on Thursday evening and end late on Monday afternoon. If you can possibly engineer your available time, try for Tuesdays, Wednesdays, and Thursdays for a trip from late March through April, or September through mid-October.

A better idea is to fish before and after the mad rush. The river holds fishable numbers of steelhead from October through May in most years. Salmon begin to show in August. These early salmon are fresh and willing if not in the dense populations that arrive a bit later. The steelhead fishing during the winter—November through early March—is quite good and you will have plenty of room.

Where can you find winter steelhead? Pretty much in the same locations as you would fish at other times, but with colder water temperatures concentrate more on deep holes and slower-current runs. Any fish eggs drifting in the current will be old and very pale. And the nymphs will be smaller than during the spring. My favorite flies are the Rotten Egg, which is a Glo Bug fly tied with 50 percent white and 50 percent Oregon cheese yarn, and a small (size 8 or 10) *Hexagenia limbata* nymph with a lot of built-in "flutter."

The water is usually very low and clear. I suggest you consider six-pound-test fluorocarbon tippet.

Hexagenia limbata *hatches are heavy
on the lower Pere Marquette.*

Double-check your knots! Fish those deep holes and slow, dark runs patiently. On the coldest days, the fish are lethargic early and late; slightly-warming water from the midday sun is often the trigger that fires activity.

There is a lot of good winter holding water downstream from the flies-only stretch. Consider a float from Rainbow Rapids to Su Lac. This is a fine stretch of river with countless deep pools, dark holes, and slower-current runs. The banks are largely held by private interests and public, walk-in access is limited. Parking is controlled by the United States Forest Service and you will need proper permits. But, nearby Baldwin, MI has as many top-notch fly-fishing guides as any town in Montana, so with just a little forethought you should have no trouble making arrangements. On my personal grading scale, many of the fly-fishing guides on the Pere Marquette are as good as any you will find anywhere. The Pere Marquette River Lodge, Baldwin Tackle, Schmidt Outfitters (Wellston), and the Troutsman (Traverse City), for starters, can help you. Top guides include (but are not limited to) John Kluesing, Walt Grau, Jac Ford, Steve Fraley, Pat Moore, John Hunter, and John Kessner.

A 9 1/2-foot rod for a 7-weight line has the right basic properties for Pere Marquette steelhead. An 8- or 9-weight is more suitable for salmon. The "PM" often forces a wading fly-angler tight to a bank and this complicates casting. Two-handed "Spey" type rods have become quite popular on the PM in recent years. The rods range from 11 to 14 feet in length and facilitate the Spey cast which, like a classic "roll cast," keeps your fly out of the bushes.

With its fame as a steelhead and salmon destination, the PM's excellent trout fishing is (relatively) lightly pressured. The river has excellent hatches of mayflies, caddis and stoneflies. All that pristine, highly-oxygenated, gravel-bottomed riffle water is perfect for a wide array of aquatic bugs. Hendricksons, Sulphurs, mahoganies, gray drakes, brown drakes, and in the lower stretches, *Hexagenia limbata,* all produce excellent dry-fly fishing during dun emergence and spinner-fall periods. Notably, the gray drake spinner falls can be spectacular, with large resident brown trout feeding aggressively.

The lower river from Branch to Walhalla, and further downstream, is silt-rich and perfect habitat for the giant *Hexagenia limbata.* The nymphs are burrowers with a two-year life span. At maturity, just before emergence, they are close to two inches in length, a substantial morsel for even a super-sized brown or rainbow. Mid to late June and into early July is the peak time for the *Hex* hatch on the PM. As on other Michigan rivers, the best fishing is during the spinner fall from early evening to full darkness. Most of the same guides that chase steelhead and salmon take fly-anglers into the slower silt-banked stretches of the PM for the nocturnal *Hex* mania. This hatch on the PM has not received the same national publicity as it has on other rivers like the Au Sable, but it is every bit as exciting and productive.

The Pere Marquette, from its headwaters near Chase through Baldwin and on downstream, is a magical river. Tributaries like the Baldwin, Little South Branch, and Big South Branch grow the PM from a small stream with carefree wading to an impressive, powerful river. The tributaries serve as spawning grounds and nurseries. Additionally they provide first-class, small-stream fly-angling for wild trout and are worthy of a visit on their own terms.

Baldwin is the best central location for a visit to the Pere Marquette. This small town has fly-shops, guide service, motels, restaurants, some shopping and is centrally located for ventures to the flies-only section, the downstream runs near Branch, or the smaller tributary waters.

Marc Linsenman hoping for a take near the Green Cottage.

Pine River

Vastly overshadowed by the larger and more famous Manistee, neighboring Pine River affords a unique fly-fishing opportunity, particularly under the federal protection afforded its lower section.

The Pine is located in the western Lower Peninsula. It courses westward through several counties and ends in the back waters of the Manistee River above Tippy Dam. Its upper reaches provide some reasonable public access at various roads and bridges that are easily identified on any good map of the area (check the *Michigan Atlas & Gazetteer* by DeLorme)

Although the upper Pine is smallish water, it is cold and fertile and produces beautiful and healthy brook, brown and rainbow trout. There are good hatches of mayflies, caddis, and stoneflies as well as sculpins, dace, shiners, and crayfish throughout the system. During non-hatch (or spinner-fall) periods, simple attractor dry-fly patterns like the Adams and Elk Hair Caddis will fool fish. The best nymphs for the upper water include Hare's Ears, Pheasant Tails, and various stonefly copies. Carry Woolly Buggers, Woolly Sculpins, and Muddler Minnows as well. Fish the pockets, undercut banks, and the timber. Trout in the Pine are quite fond of wood cover. And be sure to work the riffles thoroughly. Quite often you will find the fish of the day near the bottom of a midstream riffle. One of the best patterns to fish in the quick water is the Warbird, a hybrid Woolly Bugger adapted by Kelly Galloup. Simply add two pairs of fine rubber legs and rubber antennae to a black Woolly Bugger and you have a Warbird. It is a killing attractor when fished as a nymph in lively water.

Below Lincoln Bridge, the Pine flows 26 miles through a corridor protected by the USFS and special restrictions, remote access, and high banks. It is best to float-fish this stretch. If you have your own watercraft, you will need to obtain a special permit from the USFS. Consider a guided trip. An outfitter with the proper permits gets you to the Pine's wildest stretches (and biggest fish) in comfort. Schmidt Outfitters of Wellston holds a permit for the restricted sections of the Pine. Their professional guides use inflatable rafts with fly-angling-specific aluminum frames for a comfortable, no-kill experience on this beautiful wild river. Ray Schmidt recommends a 9-foot, 5- or 6-weight rod for all-around use on the Pine. "If you take only one rod to the Pine, this is the best choice. A 9-footer in 5- or 6-weight will have enough delicacy for dry-fly or nymph work and enough power and lift to fish streamers on a full-sinking or wet-tip line," he said.

The best hatches (and spinner falls) on the Pine include Hendricksons, Sulphurs, brown drakes, and olives. You can expect strong caddis activity throughout the season and intermittent (but very good while they last) stonefly action through late June.

Streamers are the ticket for the Pine's biggest trout. If you hire a guide, you'll be told which patterns have been most effective in the preceding days. Color seems to be one of the important features that can lose or gain favor on a daily basis. One day a yellow streamer will be hot, the next day the fish want olive or black. The consistent factor in your streamer choice is a lively, built-in, fluttering action. Take Madonnas, Rattlesnakes, Woolly Sculpins, and Zoo Cougars in white, yellow, olive, cream or tan, and black. That selection will cover all your streamer needs.

The trout in the Pine are wild and special. Afford them special care in handling, photographing, and release. Their wild, vibrant colors will capture your attention, but do not hold them too long—even the bigger fish that run over 20 inches. Take a carefully composed photo and release them gently.

The lovely and delicate Pine River flows through a protective corridor administered by the USFS.

Pine Lake

Pine Lake, near Wellston, is a jewel for fly-anglers. It has trout, panfish and northern pike.

A bit west of the Wellston village limits in Manistee County you will notice an access sign for Pine lake on M-55. It is just a short drive to some fine, underutilized fly-fishing.

This is a small, comfortable lake to fly-fish. It is easily accessible to the public and has a firm, sand boat launch and public (USFS) campground with several level and scenic camp sites. If camping is not your preference, private cottage rental is available at Pine Lake Villa, or at several motels, and at the lodge at Schmidt Outfitters in Wellston.

Pine Lake is stocked regularly with both brown and rainbow trout and some of these grow to magnum proportions. The lake also supports very large panfish and northern pike. All of these fish are valid targets for the fly-angler. The panfish love rubber-legged spider patterns, Hare's Ears, small poppers, and small, olive Woolly Buggers. The trout respond to leech patterns and minnow imitations on a sinking line. Northern pike will look for larger meals. Use 4- to 6-inch streamers in yellow and red, red and white, all white, all black, and chartreuse.

Fish the drop-offs and visible edges near the sand bars for trout. Pine Lake has excellent weed beds and lily pads that shelter northerns waiting in ambush. Early morning and late evening are usually the best times to work the weeds. Use those big streamers, or a large foam popper or deer-hair frog for aggressive pike.

This is an ideal lake for the fly-angler. It is comfortable and easy to fish with wind shelter afforded by tree-lined shores. It has obvious cover with ledges and points, weeds, drop-offs, and sand bars. One of the best places to begin fishing is right in front of the campground, just a bit to the right of the boat launch. Pine Lake is about perfect for a float tube or canoe approach. If you do not own one of these, boat rentals are available nearby.

Manistee River

The Manistee River hosts the largest steelhead runs—both fall and spring—in the Great Lakes basin.

Tiny, wild brook trout in the headwaters, Hex-slurping monster browns and rainbows in the middle reaches, and migratory trophies—steelhead, browns, salmon—below Tippy Dam are the riches of the Manistee. This beautiful river headwaters just west of the Au Sable and flows generally south, southwest, and west to its mouth at Lake Michigan at the town of Manistee.

Its upper run is classic small-stream fly-fishing. Tree- and shrub-lined shores, narrow channels, a sand-and-fine-gravel bottom with silt edges, undercut banks, beaver dams, and a mix of brookies, smallish browns and rainbows present the fly-angler with the sense of an earlier time. Short, light rods that deliver a 3-weight line, short leaders, and a handful of attractor patterns are about right. A dry-fly selection should include an Adams, Elk Hair Caddis, Lime Trude, black ant, and Royal Coachman. Nymphs can be covered with a few Gold Ribbed Hare's Ears and Pheasant Tails. Small Muddlers and Woolly Buggers, perhaps a Mickey Finn, are all the streamers you need to carry.

Obviously, if there is a hatch in progress that particular pattern should be in your vest.

Beginning at about the point where the four corners of Antrim, Kalkaska, Otsego, and Crawford counties meet south of Cty. Rd. 38, the river and its trout become more demanding. From this point on downstream to the bridge at Hwy. 72, the Manistee River gains size in both width and depth from both small feeders and ground spring flows bubbling up from the huge aquifer lying just beneath the surface. Popular access points are at Deward, Cameron Bridge, Cty. 612 bridge, and at various points along Manistee River Road.

This part of the Manistee is very popular with fly-anglers and the fish are both larger and considerably more sophisticated. Specific hatches require precise imitations for both dun and spinner-fall periods. The water is very clear and the gentle gradient allows the trout plenty of time for close inspection. Key hatches throughout the year include Hendricksons, Sulphurs, mahoganies, brown drakes, the *Hexagenia limbata*, and

BO BRINES

Isonychias. Stoneflies, including the giant *dorsata*, and caddis are also important. Hatch-specific nymphs and soft-hackled wet-fly patterns are productive. The best streamer flies will be those representing sculpins and crayfish. Be sure to check in with the local fly-shops in Grayling for accurate information on hatches and patterns. It's a reasonable bet that they will suggest low-riding parachute, Compara dun, or other lightly-hackled dun patterns for these picky fish. And, over the years they have developed a collection of spinner-phase flies that are truly excellent.

The "flies-only" stretch of the Manistee begins at the M-72 bridge and continues downstream to CCC Bridge. This is "blue-ribbon" trout water by even the strictest definition of the term. The fish grow large on abundant and varied prey. The river supports dense populations of all major aquatic insects with prolific mayfly hatches and spinner falls throughout the season. Stonefiles, caddis, dragonflies, scuds, ants, beetles, and grasshoppers are abundant. Sculpins, crayfish, dace, darters, shiners, and immature trout are actively hunted by large browns.

Equipment should be a bit heftier for this section of the Manistee. The wading angler will want a rod that can deliver large streamers as well as present a dry fly without disturbance. A 9-foot, 6-weight is a good all-around choice. With a moderately fast action, it will pound out a sinking line and bulky baitfish imitations

Steve Nevala on the "flies-only" stretch near CCC Bridge.

and, with a quick spool or reel change, a floating line and dry flies. Just about any cast in this stretch can produce a hook-up with a heavy fish whether the angler is delivering a Hendrickson, brown drake or Muddler Minnow. A rod with backbone and lifting power is helpful. Fishing from a guide's boat allows the luxury of two rods and this is the way I prefer to fish the "flies-only" stretch. I carry a 9-foot, 5-weight loaded for dry-fly work and a 9-foot (sometimes 8 1/2-foot), 6-weight rod with a full-sinking, class V line, a short, stout leader and a big sculpin pattern. In this section, there are fish large enough to scare you, large enough to stalk and eat a 14-inch trout carelessly sipping at the surface.

The real monsters in this part of the river are almost always brown trout. Some of them are caught during the brown drake hatch and every year a few skilled (and lucky) anglers report 30-inch fish during the *Hex* frenzy, but the high percentages are stacked in favor of the streamer for taking true giants. The most consistently productive streamers are the Zoo Cougar, Woolly Sculpin (in various colors), Madonna, Butt Monkey, and Trick or Treat. A four-foot leader with 10-pound-test tippet is a good idea. If the water is low and the sun bright, an eight-pound-test tippet may be necessary, but anything lighter is asking for heartache.

The long stretch of river from CCC bridge downstream through the Sharon area, past Smithville to Hodenpyle is generally and loosely referred to as "the middlegrounds." It is a large stream near Sharon and grows considerably in volume from there through the Hodenpyle stretch. Its flow (dependent upon time of year and recent precipitation) approaches 1500 cubic feet per second. The channel varies in width from 80 to 150 feet plus, and its depth ranges to 10 feet and more in certain holes and corner bends. The flow can be rapid and heavy and first-time visitors need to exercise common sense. Under no circumstances should you fish here at night without first exploring and carefully noting your selected area's boundaries during daylight hours. This stretch of the Manistee is serious business with enough "giants" (trout over 25 inches) to embarrass a lot of western rivers. In my opinion, it is the best trophy-trout water east of the Rocky Mountains, and by any measure, one of the top seven or eight in the country. It has plenty of access for the wading angler throughout. Just check the country maps and explore a bit if so inclined, but I recommend a guided float trip as the best (by far) method to approach this water. Guides from the Troutsman, in Traverse City, and from Schmidt Outfitters, in Wellston, will provide comfort, knowledge, and every

Upper Manistee brown trout love cone-head Woolly Sculpins.

angling advantage whether you are casting *Hex* flies into the midnight gloom or pounding big streamers during the day.

The section through Hodenpyle is wild and beautiful. There are hardwood ridges, cedar swamps, frothing riffles, mirror-like pools, abundant wildlife, and

A favored bend for guides and clients on the "flies-only" stretch.

brilliantly colored, wild trout. Be sure to include a good camera with your gear. You may want to photograph an eagle, mink, or fawn. You will surely want to capture images of that hook-jawed brown cradled gently before release.

Perhaps the most famous run of the Manistee is the final push from Tippy Dam to Lake Michigan. This fame (some would say "infamy") is due to the river's incredible runs of salmonids from Lake Michigan. Pacific salmon start to appear in late August and the ensuing big-fish frenzy runs through early October. chinook salmon in excess of 30 pounds are relatively commonplace and this fact attracts people—lots of people. And there are some sub-humans thrown into the mix, creatures that snag fish and litter. In order to retain my reputation as a fair and objective individual, I'll just refer to them as scum, or ditch pigs.

The best way to fish ethically for salmon below Tippy is to float, and the best way to float is with a guide who can get you to those areas where the fish are receptive to the fly. A nymph drifted below an indicator will produce fair-hooked salmon that put on magnificent runs, leaps, and have tremendous power. You won't "hook" as many fish as the ditch pig, but you can look in the mirror without cringing.

Happily, the Manistee's best fall steelhead angling comes after the salmon frenzy has subsided. This is an incredible run of rock-hard, brilliant, highly-energized trout. They are upstream to eat and that is a very good thing indeed. These steelhead range from two to twenty pounds with eight pounds being a fair guess at average.

When hooked they are frantic—a series of wild explosions in the form of very fast runs punctuated with awesome leaps. They are heart-pounders and it takes good tackle to do them justice. A 9 1/2- or 10-foot rod for a 7- or 8-weight line will have the backbone to settle issues quickly enough so that your fish can be released unharmed. A smooth, disc-drag real with at least 150 yards of backing is appropriate. Although the fall run of steelhead is continually presented with drifting salmon and brown trout eggs, you will find nymph patterns to be as effective as egg flies. Caddis nymphs, Pheasant Tails, Hare's Ears, *limbata* nymphs, stonefly nymphs, and Woolly Buggers are favorites for fall steelhead as well as for the large brown trout on their late-fall spawning run from Lake Michigan.

Steelhead remain in the lower Manistee throughout the cold winter months. As the days lengthen and the water beings to warm slightly in March, the numbers of fish grow considerably. By mid-April, the Manistee holds more steelhead than most west coast rivers. The run numbers in the many thousands and is a mix of wild (born-in-the-river) and hatchery fish. The hatchery fish are easily identified by their clipped fins. It was earlier estimated that the hatchery plants would make up approximately 60 percent of the run, but I think that estimate is too high. My guess is that at least half the run is wild.

The same general tackle recommendations apply to the spring fishery. It is my opinion that 5- and 6-weight rods are too light to contest powerful fish in big, heavy water and provide steelhead a fair chance at recovery and survival. Egg flies and nymphs take 90-plus percent of the fly-caught steelhead in the Manistee.

Outfitter Ray Schmidt searching for early fall steelhead below Tippy Dam.

But under the right conditions, swinging Spey patterns, classic west coast flies, and streamers will bring arm-jolting strikes.

The Manistee is about a two-hour drive from my house. I own a drift boat and am familiar with the water below Tippy, but I always hire a guide (or trade a guided day on the Au Sable) when I fish that part of the river. The fly-fishing guides who work that water are very good.

You might be surprised below Tippy. Huge walleyes are present during the spring run of steelhead. And you might see a sturgeon nosing over the gravel. The sturgeon are huge, ominous, pre-historic, rare, and endangered. Do not cast to them. Just look and be thankful...

A classic, aggressive fall fish that ate a Hex nymph.

Lake Dubonnet

Just a few miles southwest of northern Michigan's largest city, Lake Dubonnet is within a short drive of the glittering coast and toney golf shrines of Traverse City. It is easily reached by taking Highway 31 south and west to the county line between Grand Traverse and Benzie where a right turn on Gonder Road leads directly to the boat-launch site on this scenic and productive lake.

Dubonnet is in a wild setting; there is a campground but no cabins and the feeling, despite the proximity to thousands of people, is that one has fallen back in time or been deposited somewhere in northern Canada. The lake's north end is studded with a wild array of timber and is pancaked with beds of weeds and lily pads. Its eastern shore has small islands, tall ridges and a handsome skyline of hardwoods.

This small lake (about 180 acres) is crammed full with panfish, largemouth bass, and northern pike.

An average-sized bluegill for Lake Dubonnet.

Many of the fish are small but there are plenty of trophies available. The water is food-rich and well-oxygenated, and the weeds provide ample cover for prey and predator alike. The clear, open-water pockets between the weed beds are ideal spots to drop a long, slinky streamer for northerns or a Yuk Bug or leech pattern for bass.

On a recent visit to Dubonnet I fished with Russ Maddin and Kelly Galloup, both of Traverse City. Russ is an accomplished, young fly-fishing guide and Kelly owns The Troutstman, arguably one of the most complete fly-shops in the state. Both men are (obviously) highly-skilled fly-anglers and it was both a pleasure and a learning experience to watch them place their casts into tiny openings and work their retrieves at various seductive speeds.

The fishing was a bit slow that particular day. We had been delayed in our start by a variety of circumstances and did not hit the water until nearly two in the afternoon on a bright, cloudless hot day. Still, the precision casts (Kelly's and Russ'—not mine) brought some heavy wakes out from under the pads and from the bases of long-dead tree stumps. Some were large bass, others were trophy northerns, but they did not pursue far from their cover. The bright sky and clear water seemed to make them hesitant, but it was exciting enough just to see them and the push of water they created as they followed the fly. We did catch some respectable bluegills on small nymphs and a few small largemouth bass on a variety of patterns including the five-inch-long gaudy streamers intended for northerns.

Kelly and Russ recommended red-and-white and yellow-and-red streamers of the Deceiver type for pike. They should feature some tinsel or Krystal Flash for added zip, and the hooks must be needle-sharp. Both men use a shock tippet of 30-pound-test Maxima and will rotate between floating and sinking lines to complement their strategies for various depths. Six-weight rods are acceptable for most occasions, but both suggested an 8-weight for the large fish around the weeds and stumps.

Dubonnet is a beautiful lake, generally sheltered from the wind, a quiet slice of wilderness only twenty minutes from some of the most prestigious shops and most challenging golf courses in the nation.

Grand Traverse Bay

A small steelhead (about 20 inches) from Grand Traverse Bay.

The land mass surrounded by the Great Lakes on three sides forms the shape of a left-hand mitten. This is instantly recognized worldwide as Michigan's Lower Peninsula. In telephone conversations with geographically disadvantaged folks (those that do not live in or close to Michigan) a question that is often asked is "Where is Oscoda county? Is it near the 'thumb' or 'little finger'?" The "little finger" is the sheltering point of land jutting north into Lake Michigan that protects the waters of Grand Traverse Bay's east and west arms from the storms of the big water. My answer is usually, "70 miles east of the 'little finger'."

Northern Michigan's largest community, Traverse City, sits at the south end of the bay. On the west side of town, the Leelanau Peninsula (little finger) juts north. In the center of town, Old Mission Peninsula lies north to south and separates the West Arm from the East Arm of the bay. On the east edge of town, Michigan's main land mass winds north to the "tip of the mitt" at the Straits of Mackinac. The total shoreline of Grand Traverse Bay exceeds 130 miles. The sustaining watershed is over 970 square miles with clear, clean streams, rolling hills, deep forests, prosperous farms, orchards, and vineyards covering six counties.

The bay has 39 species of fish and a maximum depth, in its East Arm, of 600 feet. Lake trout, coho and chinook salmon, brown trout, steelhead, smallmouth bass, northern pike, and carp are the main species of interest to fly-anglers. Of these, the salmonids and smallmouth bass attract the most attention. Northern pike, for the most part, are less

The bass grow very large in Grand Traverse Bay.

often a target species and catches seem to be almost incidental for fly-rodders seeking salmon, large trout, and bass.

Russ Maddin is a young fly-fishing guide who works for the Troutsman in Traverse City. More than anyone else I know, Russ stalks the flats of Grand Traverse Bay and Lake Michigan from Northport to the mouth of the Platte River. He fishes hard and throughout the year for trout, salmon, bass and "whatever else wants to eat my fly."

Russ recommends either 9- or 9 1/2-foot, 8-weight rods with backbone enough to fight the wind and outmuscle large fish. He feels that 175 yards of backing is the minimum required and that a solid, smooth reel is mandatory. Russ likes the Scientific Angler "Stillwater" line because it is a clear, slow sinker and resists coiling in cold water.

Early in the year, prey items are smaller than later in the season, so use 2- to 4-inch Clousers in white and olive and white and chartreuse. They have a great silhouette and, when tied with Ultra Hair, are extremely durable and life-like. Also carry a few poppers and sliders with tan heads and white marabou tails, and some crayfish patterns such as the Trick or Treat. As the season progresses and the water warms, the prey species grow and your patterns should be scaled up in size.

Although there are spots with deep water tight to the shore, the vast majority of Grand Traverse Bay's shoreline is a series of flats. From the air, these flats with their clear water over light sand are reminiscent of the out islands of the Bahamas—simply beautiful.

As you explore, you will want to look for five basic types of flats. These hold the widest variety and highest concentrations of game fish. *Rock flats* are covered with rocks ranging from golf ball to basketball size. They produce outstanding fishing early in the year. Large brown trout and steelhead actively hunt crayfish on these flats and chunky smallmouth are always close by. *Patch flats* feature isolated patches of rock through an extensive reach of sand. These rock islands provide excellent cover amid the barrens and are good for all fish all year long. *Sand ridge flats* are all sand, but with an upwelling ridge and a depth change on both sides. These act as thoroughfares. Game fish prowl the edges of the highways looking for food. *Internal trough flats* have very good fly-angling almost at the shoreline. They are recognizable by a trough with 2-3 feet of deeper water bisecting a sand reach. They are often only 30 to 50 feet from shore and can often be fished without getting your feet wet. These fish highways are most common on the Lake Michigan side from Northport south to the mouth of the Platte River. *Multiple trough flats* present a series of troughs separated by a series of sandbars. They often extend out into the lake or bay for a considerable distance and some care needs to be exercised while fishing them. Be prepared for a variety of fish from these flats. Salmon, steelhead, brown trout, and lake trout travel and feed along them on a regular basis.

There is a lot of water here to explore. On the east side of the East Arm, from Acme to Elk Rapids, look close to the mouths of Mitchell Creek, Acme Creek, and Yuba Creek as starting points. You will find a lot of sand and rock combinations. Start with crayfish patterns and small Clouser Minnows. The west side of East Arm features relatively narrow flats with exterior

Russ Maddin shoots a long line for cruisers on Grand Traverse Bay.

the fly-angler. And, it is huge. From Grand Traverse Light at the Leelanau State Park at the tip of the peninsula, through Cathead Bay, Peterson Park, the town of Leeland, Good Harbor, the Sleeping Bear Dunes National Lake Shore, to the mouth of the Platte River, it is very lightly fished with a long rod and flies. It is an untapped resource with tremendous populations of aggressive salmonid species.

Grand Traverse Bay has such high-quality fly-fishing over such a large area that it would be impossible to cover it all in several seasons let alone do it justice as part of a small book. In addition to what I have referred to here, there are numerous quality inland lakes and wonderful trout streams close by. The lakes include Torch, Charlevoix, Leelanau, Long Lake, Dubonnet, Glen, Platte, and Crystal. Rivers like the Betsie, Platte, Boardman, Jordan, and others have excellent stream trout fishing and substantial runs of steelhead and salmon.

When exploring and fishing the flats of Grand Traverse Bay and Lake Michigan, consider using a weather radio. Pay close attention to wind direction. You will want to know if a wind shift will hurt or help. A change in direction might mean a push of warm water to the location you are going to fish. This is a good thing.

A variety of "low-light" patterns for steelhead.

troughs. These are more difficult to fish and wade as the fish are farther out from the shore. The east side of West Arm has lots of rock flats and superb fly-angling for lakers, browns, salmon, and smallmouth, but there is limited, easy public access. The best place to start is at Old Mission Point. The west side of West Arm has probably the best and most varied fly angling opportunities. It has classic flats fishing—beautiful, clear water, a wide range of types of flats, and all gamefish species. You can start right at the mouth of the Boardman River in downtown Traverse City and work your way north along the shore to Sutton's Bay. You will find eager, electric steelhead, massive brown trout, lake trout, and aggressive salmon throughout this section. The Lake Michigan side is really not part of the bay at all; it is obviously outside the bay sheltered by the Leelanau Peninsula. It is, however, a wild paradise for

When you are wading the flats, move very slowly and watch carefully. The fish are most often visible and, like bonefishing in the Bahamas, this is part of the appeal. If you work slowly and carefully, you are less likely to spook fish and push them out to deep water.

Traverse City is a lovely town with friendly folks and every conceivable luxury to complement the necessary. Fine shopping and dining, scenic vistas, and world-class golf courses are just a part of the community's attractions.

III

East Coast Region

This is the "sunrise side" of Michigan's Lower Peninsula. The best fishing runs from a loose southern border near Bay City north to Mackinaw City. The eastern boundary is Lake Huron's shoreline and the western line is I-75. That is a lot of territory. All of it is dotted with lakes and ponds and ribboned by rivers and streams.

Michigan's most constant feature is water—the world's largest lakes, medium-sized lakes, delicate ponds, big rivers, and fragile streams. A request for directions to someplace on the east side will likely bring a response close to, "Well, you take the county road around Jake's Pond, then turn right at Bass Lake Drive. Go about 2 miles—you'll cross two bridges over Gilchrist Creek—and take a left on Sam's Pond Drive. It's on the left."

The following is a small sampling of the waters where I learned to fly-fish and that remain some of my favorite places.

Beyond what is covered here, consider the following from south to north—Crooked Lake in Clare County for bass and northerns, Pratt Lake in Gladwin County for bass and panfish, Lake St. Helen in Roscommon County for northerns, panfish, and bass, Shupac Lake in Crawford County for trout and smallmouth, the East Branch of the Au Gres River in Iosco County for steelhead, the Black, Sturgeon, and Pigeon rivers near Vanderbilt and Wolverine for trout, and the Ocqueoc River west of Rogers City for steelhead and salmon.

Lake George (*Ogemaw County*)

Kelly Neuman fishes along a drop-off near a weed bed on Lake George.

There are two bodies of water named Lake George within thirty-five miles of each other. One is a few miles northwest of the town of Clare in Clare County, but the object of this recommendation is the smaller lake just five miles south of West Branch, the county seat of Ogemaw County.

Access is easy. The most direct route from West Branch is south on Cook Road (this is Exit 212 on Interstate 75) about three miles to Channel Lake Road, then west on Channel Lake Road to the well-marked public access and boat-launch area.

Lake George is exceptionally clean, clear, and cool with a diversified target mix for the fly-rod angler. Crappies, bluegills, perch, largemouth bass, northern pike, rainbow trout and carp are all available along the weedline at the edge of the sandflats or in the deeper pockets during the heat of the day.

The best approach for a mixed bag on the fly is to proceed clockwise around the lake from the public access. Start your boat or float tube a few feet off (on the deep side) the edge of the shelf where weeds and dark water start to blend with the shallows. Make your casts toward shore and place the fly at varying distances between the bank, weed beds, and the drop-off. A slow twitch retrieve has worked well with nymphs and small wets for large bluegills. A more erratic, jerky retrieve with Yuk Bugs, Trick or Treats, and Woolly Buggers produces hefty bass and some northerns. Streamers, *big ones* for northerns and small white Clousers for crappie, work best in front of a moderate-density sinking-tip line.

Floaters work as well. Large, deer-hair bugs in frog or mouse configurations will attract both bass and northerns early in the morning or late in the day. Small cricket, 'hopper, and rubber-legged spider patterns will take the panfish and smaller bass.

Early and late in the season when the water is cool, large rainbow trout (to 20 inches and some larger) cruise the edges and look for dragonfly and damselfly nymphs. They will also inhale black Woolly Buggers, Mohair leeches, and a variety of streamers. Try patterns like Doc's Glass Eye Minnow,

This aggressive little sunfish hit a Zoo Cougar intended for bass.

a white-and-olive Clouser, or a white Marabou Muddler for best results. These trout are thick bodied and very robust. Despite the clear water, a tippet strength of about six pounds is about as light as is practical. And there's always the chance of hooking a large northern on a cast intended for rainbows.

Carp between six and twenty pounds cruise the sand flats slowly or suspend motionless in less than three feet of water. They are extremely wary and will spook violently if a clumsy cast lands too near. More frustrating is their tendency to slowly move out of harm's way when even a clean, gentle delivery lands too close. This is like fishing the Florida flats for bonefish or permit. Ultra-clear water and a demanding quarry require precise casting and a stealthy approach. Small nymphs (size 8-10) like Hare's Ears, dragonflies, philoplume Hex, and drab soft-hackles are required. Classic bonefish flies like the Crazy Charlie (in tan or olive) stir up the bottom with small puffs of mud. The carp like this.

Northern pike and largemouth bass prowl the heavy aquatic vegetation in ambush.

Carp are gaining in popularity for good reason. They are powerful, very fast, and picky. They have stamina enough to severely test a high percentage of anglers. If you want a challenge, if you like drama and high-speed chases, give them a fair try. You won't be disappointed.

Lake George is a delightful venue for a mixed bag with the potential for a trophy bluegill, bass, northern, trout, or carp.

Londo Lake

This is one of the lakes that local anglers have made a favorite for large fish, particularly northern pike. The pike are joined by healthy populations of large bluegills and largemouth bass. And all three species can be reasonably expected by fly-rod anglers exploring the lake by tube, canoe, or boat.

There are actually two Londo Lakes, West Londo and East Londo, nestled on the county line between southern Ogemaw and Iosco counties. West Londo Lake actually straddles the county line. It is surrounded by cabins and private homes while East Londo Lake has private dwellings only on its west shore. East Londo's eastern shore is wild and beautiful and this is the lake the local experts target for large fish.

There is a small public access and boat launch on the west side of East Londo. It takes a bit of meandering to find this access and (probably) the easiest approach is from the small town of Hale on Curtis Road past a large, left-hand curve. You will pass a small store, then 2.5 miles farther you will find a small gravel road. Turn left and drive about one third of a mile to the public access which is marked by a small sign.

East Londo is small (about 90 acres) and easy enough to cover thoroughly either in the morning or evening. It has clean, clear water and extensive weed cover punctuated with fallen trees, points, and grassy banks.

I recommend that for your first trip to East Londo, you fish it with a friend. One angler should start with either a Hare's Ear or small Woolly Worm for the large bluegills while the second angler throws a red-and-white Deceiver, or chartreuse Dahlberg Diver for northerns. The bass will hit either or both and,

dependent upon success, both anglers can then adapt to the preference of the day. On my last visit to Londo Lake I fished with Kelly Neuman, a fly-fishing guide and rod-builder. It was a hot, clear day in the middle of one of the worst dry spells in this state's history. The large bass and northerns were sulking deep but we had a fine time with smaller fish and caught some handsome panfish. One exceptionally aggressive bluegill ate a large pike streamer nearly the fish's equal in length. During the course of that late morning we had the pleasure of watching a pair of loons, several hen mallards leading their puffball young, herons, and a majestic bald eagle that watched us with a baleful eye.

East Londo is quiet and the east shore is serene. It has a wilderness feel to it despite the fact that it is in the heart of "vacation country." I have not seen jet ski or water ski activity on the lake and that is another definite plus to East Londo Lake.

Below left: Casting for pike and bass near the weeds on East Londo Lake.

Below: The eastern shore of Londo Lake is wild and scenic.

Rifle River Recreation Area

The beautiful, clear lakes within the Rifle River Recreation Area receive light angling pressure.

Nestled within the boundaries of the Au Sable State Forest, this several-thousand-acre wilderness recreation area is just four miles east of Rose City and about 190 miles north of Detroit. This expansive tract was once owned by the early auto manufacturer, H.M. Jewett and was operated as a private fishing and hunting preserve named "Grousehaven." The property was acquired by the Department of Conservation in 1945 and was operated as a research facility until 1963 when it was transferred to the Parks Division.

The area has 11 lakes and ponds and several miles of excellent trout streams. No motors, including electric, are allowed on the lakes and ponds. This ensures quiet and enhances the feeling of a remote, wilderness angling experience.

To strengthen the wilderness solitude, there are five rustic cabins available for rent that are some distance removed from one large, major campground and three rustic campgrounds. The 80-site modern camping facility has a swimming beach, playground, boat launch, and an RV pump-out station. The three rustic facilities accommodate a total of 101 campers. These sites have limited facilities. The area is open all year and its 14 miles of trails and pathways offer hiking, crosscountry skiing, and snow-shoeing.

It may be because of the "no motor" restriction, but the fishing pressure on the lakes is minimal when compared to most others with reasonable public access. And the fly-fishing pressure is almost nil. I live only 11 miles from this jewel and over the last 10 years have only seen a handful of other fly-anglers (and only *one* float tube) on the lakes. To say that these beautiful, clean lakes and ponds are underexplored for fly-fishing is pure understatement.

The two largest lakes within the area are Devoe and Grousehaven. Both have ramps for small boat launching and feature strong trout populations as the main angling opportunity.

Devoe Lake is the larger of the two. It has panfish and bass and a few walleyes, but rainbow trout are the most notable species in the lake. Large rainbows in excess of 20 inches will cruise the beautiful clear edges along the bays on the lake's northwest side early and late in the year and at dawn and dusk during summer's heat. Because of the clear water, a quiet approach and accurate casting is required. The larger fish spook quickly if a heavy fly splashes down too closely, or if an errant cast drops a shadow over them. Long leaders, at least 10 feet, and fine tippets will help. Cast well ahead of the prowling fish. Try to drop the fly six to eight feet in front and give it a twitch. Wet patterns should be twitched back slowly. Use nymphs with philoplume tails and gills for added life-like action, and marabou streamers and Woolly Buggers.

Grousehaven Lake has both brown and rainbow trout as well as panfish and a few northern pike. It should be fished in much the same manner as Devoe.

Gamble Creek is a rarely-fished jewel with wild brook and brown trout.

The water is just as clear and the trout just as nervous and intolerant of careless presentation. There is a boat ramp on the northwest corner of the lake with ample parking for several vehicles.

Directly southwest from the boat ramp and about halfway across the lake, there are two deep water pockets that descend to 50 feet. During the warmest weather, the trout shelter in these pockets and are generally inaccessible to the fly-angler. But, during cooler periods, both browns and rainbows cruise and feed throughout the lake. In general, Grousehaven is fairly well sheltered from high winds and regardless of direction, there will always be a quiet cove or shore that is leeward.

A favorite tactic here it to use a large, philoplume Hex nymph with a small Hare's Ear as a dropper. From your tube, boat, or canoe, cast *out*ward and retrieve slowly back toward the shoreline. Another good technique for Grousehaven employs a mink or rabbit fur strip leech with a pale yellow body. This fly does double duty in that it represents both a leech and a nightcrawler.

Grebe, Lodge, and Jewett are smaller lakes but each has a public access. Lost Lake, Mallard Pond, and Scaup Lake require a short hike to reach. They are smaller and receive extremely light angling pressure. Carry a small assortment of flies including the Hare's Ear and rubber-legged spiders for panfish, a few poppers, and an assortment of Woolly Buggers in various colors and you'll be well prepared on these smaller lakes.

There is a lot of moving water within the Rifle River Recreation Area and the most notable is the park's namesake—the Rifle River. It headwaters at the outflow from Devoe Lake just a few yards upstream from its bridge at Ranch Road. This is a premier trout stream with brook trout, brown trout, rainbow trout, and seasonally strong runs of steelhead, Pacific salmon, and large brown trout ascending on spawning runs from Lake Huron. It is open to angling throughout the year. Coverage of the Rifle beyond the recreation area's boundaries follows later in this book.

The Rifle has excellent mayfly hatches throughout its course from Devoe Lake to the park's southern boundary and beyond. Significant hatches of olives, Hendricksons, March browns, Sulphurs, brown drakes, *Isonychia*, and others produce excellent dry-fly fishing. Caddis, stoneflies, crayfish, sculpins, dace, shiners, immature lampreys, and the odd, bad-luck field mouse present a varied, protein-rich food base for trout.

Much of the upper section of the river is relatively narrow with deep silt edges and heavily-wooded banks. The water is clean and cold. Care should be exercised while wading—watch out for tangles of stumps and logs under the surface and for areas with a soft muck bottom. A 4- or 5-weight rod is ideal for the stream trout, but a heavier fly-rod is needed for steelhead (they average about seven pounds) in the spring and for salmon (average 17 pounds) in the fall.

Downstream from the Ranch Road bridge, past the "whirlpool" and about halfway to the Ranch Campground, Houghton Creek enters the Rifle from the west. Houghton is a fine fly-fishing trout stream in its own right and supports some hefty brown trout throughout the season. But, unlike the Rifle, it is not open all year. Be sure to check the fishing regulations for legal dates.

This lovely stream has all the same hatches as the Rifle. In addition, it is a fine venue for terrestrials. Cricket, ant, and especially grasshopper patterns produce handsome, highly-colored browns throughout the summer. Immediately after the season opener, until about May 10, there will be "drop-back" steelhead in the lower Houghton. These are spent, or spawned-out, fish on their way back to the Rifle and then to Lake Huron. Again in the fall, before the traditional closing at the end of September, trophy migrants nose into the Houghton at the confluence with the Rifle. More than a few salmon and large browns spawn in the upper Houghton, so be prepared.

Gamble Creek is a small, heavily-wooded stream that crosses Ranch Road just a short distance west of the park's entrance. It offers "creep and crawl" fly-angling for wild trout that rarely see a fly. These are very tight quarters. The creek is rarely 10 feet wide and has heavy overhangs of cedar, balsam, fir, and pine. You *will* lose a few flies. So what? The fish are rare gems and well worth the effort. Attractor patterns, both wet and dry, are all that is needed. A few Royal Trudes, Humpies, an Adams or two, and a Mickey Finn, maybe a Woolly Bugger or Muddler Minnow make a pretty complete selection of flies for Gamble Creek.

The fly-fishing opportunities within the Rifle River Recreation Area are more than one can sample in a season, let alone a short visit. And there is more than I have covered here. A combination hunting/fly-fishing trip in the fall can be wonderful. The Rifle River and most of the lakes are open to angling all year. The fall adds the spectacular colors of the hardwoods to cool water, aggressive fish, and the flush of woodcock and grouse.

A pass is required. The daily fee is $4.00, but the annual tab is only $20.00. This is one of the best bargains in the entire state.

The Rifle River

A late-March steelhead about to be returned to the Rifle River.

From its headwaters in the Rifle River Recreation Area at the small village of Lupton, to its mouth at Lake Huron, the Rifle River's flow is unimpeded by dams. Steelhead, salmon, and large lake-dwelling brown trout make their seasonal ascensions through a course of 60-plus river miles to the gravel runs and riffles in the rolling, mixed forest and farm land of Ogemaw County. It is estimated that it takes these rushing spawners less than two days to reach the gravel near the State Road bridge at Selkirk. It takes a fly-angler less than three hours to reach the same spot from downtown Detroit.

This is a small river with limited public access throughout its course. But that limited access is well located, in a strategic sense, for a pretty fair percentage of the prime steelhead, salmon, and brown trout water. For the most part, knowledgeable anglers concentrate efforts between Greenwood Road on the downstream end and Sage Lake Road at the upper end. Several bridges cross the stream in this reach and these are easily located with any decent map.

Anglers and pressure are, of course, concentrated in close proximity to the obvious public access points but, if you are willing to hike out of range, you will almost always find peaceful angling, if not total solitude, even on weekends at the peak of the various seasons for the large trophies. However, the best way to achieve success is to float this little river—quietly.

Public launch sites are few and far between—either too close or too distant for an ideal day on the stream, and private facilities are closely guarded and on a fee basis. Contact Bachelder Spool & Fly in Rose City and book a float. The guides there have made the necessary arrangements for convenient, productive trips and they know the river intimately.

The steelhead in this beautiful little river average about seven pounds, or 26 inches. The range is from about 22 to 36 inches, maybe a bit larger. In the spring of 1999 we saw several (and hooked, but did not land two) that would push 40 inches. We guessed their weight in excess of 23 pounds.

Peak times for spring steelhead are the middle two weeks of April, but this varies a bit from year to year.

They seem to come in three distinct waves, centering their spawning activity in slightly different sections of the river. Another complication comes from the hordes of red horse and white suckers that ascend the Rifle each spring. When the suckers are "in" it is difficult to drift a nymph without catching one. And, it seems, the steelhead just do not like to be around them. *Mykiss* tend to fade, drop back, and shut down until the suckers leave.

Late August brings the first of the Pacific salmon (kings) into the lower Rifle. By early September, the run from Greenwood Road upstream to beyond Sage Lake Road has fishable numbers ranging from 10 to 30 pounds plus. When these salmon are still fresh they can be a real heart-pounding rush. It is best to fish for

This magnificent 32-inch buck steelhead ate a tiny nymph in low, clear water.

When the leaves turn, the Rifle hosts runs of salmon, brown trout and steelhead from Lake Huron.

them under low-light conditions and dawn has been traditionally better than dusk. Marabou Spey patterns like the Popsicle and Tequila Sunrise are effective, but most salmon are caught on nymph and egg copies. The Yuk Bug, Girdle Bug, Hare's Ear, and Hex nymphs produce very well. Include some large pheasant tail and green caddis patterns along with an assortment of Glo Bugs and you're well equipped.

Steelhead and spawning browns make their fall appearance by mid-November. These are rock-hard fish that are aggressive and wary at the same time. They will eat your fly, but will not tolerate careless presentations. Pale egg patterns, Woolly Buggers, Zoo Cougars, and an assortment of nymphs—caddis, black stoneflies, Hex (in small sizes:

10, 12), and Hare's Ears are all that is needed.

Resident trout fishing is quite good on the Rifle. It supports healthy populations of both brown and rainbows as well as a few wildly-colored brookies. Most rainbows fall in the 8- to 14-inch range while the browns get much larger. Each year several resident browns are taken in the 10-pound class. The brookies are small, wild, and delicate rarely exceeding 12 inches. They should be handled with *extreme* care and immediately released. They are beautiful and as dumb as a box of rocks. Any living creature with those two descriptors must rely on us for their continuance.

The Rifle has excellent hatches of caddis, stoneflies, and mayflies. These all bring outstanding dry-fly

Guide Mike Bachelder searching for lake-run brown trout near the State Road access.

Michigan Blue-Ribbon Fly-Fishing Guide

Resident brown trout are partial to large streamers on cloudy days.

action. My favorite bugs on the Rifle are the Hendricksons, March browns, and brown drakes. Additionally, there are olives, *Isonychia*, Cahills, and in the lower reaches, white flies (*Ephoron leukon*).

An assortment of nymphs for the Rifle should include the basics plus a few of the following—Princes, Zug Bugs, bead-head caddis, and stoneflies. Sculpin and crayfish patterns are a must for the streamer-angler, as are black Zonkers, olive Woolly Buggers, and cream-and-yellow cone-head marabous.

Matching the hatch is in order for dry-fly work. When no emergence or spinner fall is apparent, try terrestrials. Ants, crickets, and hoppers work well. General attractor patterns like the Royal Wulff, Lime Trude, Humpy, Irresistibles, and (of course) the

Adams all produce. Throw in a few stonefly patterns from size 10 to 4 in tan, yellow, and black. Lastly, I always carry a couple of deer-hair mice with long, black marabou tails.

This little river is a lot better than good. It has fine angling for stream trout and what can be honestly classed as true "Blue-Ribbon" fly-fishing for magnificent steelhead, salmon, and migratory brown trout. Its only drawbacks are 1. limited access (this may actually be its savior due to its size). This is countered by hiring a guide. Drawback 2. Heavy canoe traffic in the summer months during mid day.

For current conditions and projected opportunity, contact Bachelder Spool & Fly (address and phone number in Resources).

The Loon Lake Group

TOM BUHR

A typical Island Lake bluegill.
Left: Island Lake has a healthy bass population.

Large rainbows die of old age in Crater Lake. Very few see a fly during their lifetime. Nestled into a small glacial roll of "sink holes" and hills at the southern edge of Oscoda County, Crater and its two larger sister lakes—Island and Loon—are accessed off County Road 486 between Rose City and Mio. All three are bordered, at least in part, by the Huron National Forest.

Crater Lake is aptly named. It sits in a circular bowl at the bottom of a very steep slope. The heavily wooded

incline is at an angle close to 60 degrees and the water's surface is about 150 feet below the small parking area. Crater is surrounded by federal property. There are no cabins, no docks, no services. Thankfully, there is a sturdy, wide, wooden stairway—complete with "switch backs" and rest areas—that negotiates the precipitous slope.

Two *strong* people with good lungs could probably wrestle a canoe down and up the stairs (note— watercraft may *not* be left overnight!), but this small pond is best explored from a belly boat or similar craft. It is only a few acres and nearly a perfect circle; it can be navigated completely and thoroughly by tube in just a couple of hours.

A few small children fish Crater from shore with their parents around the major holidays. Otherwise, angling pressure is almost non-existent. Its rainbows grow very large; probably (only a guess) less than 100 fish are taken during a season and it is regularly stocked. I have seen many fish over 25 inches cruising the shoreline as they complete a circular tour of the pond.

The namesake bird of Loon Lake. This photo was taken near a steep ledge that holds large rainbow trout.

Crater has caddis, mayflies, dobsonflies, damsel- and dragonflies. Heavy hatches can occur at dusk in late May and June. If you time it right, you are in for a royal treat. If no hatch is evident (bulging trout circling the lake's shore in pods), fish a sinking line with nymphs and leech patterns. Woolly Buggers in black or olive are always a good choice. Dragonfly nymphs, flat-bodied in olive and dark brown, and damselfly patterns are productive. The best mayfly nymph patterns will have fluttering philoplume tails and gills. Fish them with a slow, hand-twist retrieve and distinct pauses and starts.

Loon Lake is just on the other side of Cty. 486 from the entrance to Crater. It is a much larger body of water, about 140 acres, and is blessed with a series of sheltered, deep-water coves, steep drop-offs, drowned timber, and clean, cold water.

Largemouth bass, panfish, and rainbow trout are the main attractions for the fly-angler. The bass grow very large for this latitude as do bluegills (to 11 inches) and yellow perch (15 inches). Rainbows are stocked yearly and grow to impressive size.

During the early season, bass, trout, and bluegills covet the clear shallows and they can be seen easily as they cruise along the shoreline. The trout prefer leech and nymph patterns and, occasionally, a small white streamer. The bass respond well to leech flies and surface bug—a deer-hair frog is a consistent producer. Panfish are greedy for nymphs, small Woolly Buggers (size 10), and a wet Royal Coachman. The Royal Coachman seems to work even more effectively after its white wings have been chewed off. I now carry a few tied (deliberately) without the wings.

There is one public access on Loon Lake, a USFS picnic ground and beach on Cty. 486 about one quarter mile from M-33. Canoes, small boats, and tubes can be carried from the parking lot to the water, but they may not be left overnight.

Island Lake is where I caught my first bluegill on a fly-rod—and my first largemouth bass. The memory is clear. It was a warm Saturday morning in May. My father and I sat in his little green duck boat about forty yards out from the shore in front of our cabin. He was showing me how to cast (he was a patient man) and I lathered the surface a bit. The first fish was a bluegill that ate a little yellow rubber spider. I remember yelling at my mother who was watching us from the wooden swing near the dock. "Look! Mom, look!" She waved. The next fish was a bass of about 14 inches. It pulled much harder and jumped. I was afraid I would drop the rod and clamped *both* hands with all my might. My dad lipped the bass and held it up, showing it to my mother who clapped and smiled. Bass season was not yet open and he released the fish. The sun was shining. My dad mussed my hair. I was six years old.

This small lake of about 70 acres has some extremely large bluegills and bass that have a penchant for cruising in shallow water—even during the dog days of August—early in the morning and late in the evening. This is a lake that is easy to fish with a gradual slope to depth. No motors are allowed on Island Lake and this adds considerably to the calm, relaxed feeling that always comes over me when I fish there.

Out of a sense of nostalgia, I fish the area near the public beach while wading, but it's a good bet that a float tube approach or a canoe would be a bit more productive. There is no public launch site for boats, but canoes can be hand carried to the water from the parking lot of the US Forest Service campground (a very nice campground) off Cty. 486.

Take a selection of small poppers, rubber spiders, and a Hare's Ear or three for panfish. The bass love *big*, black Woolly Buggers, mink leeches, and deer-hair bugs.

Big Creek Preserve

A large rainbow starts a run on Beaver Flats Pond.

There are two stream- and spring-fed ponds nestled among the oak ridges, woodduck sloughs, and grouse coverts of Big Creek Preserve a few miles south of Mio in Oscoda County.

Just a few hundred yards west of the intersection of Zimowske Road (County Road 489) and Michigan Highway 33, Big Creek Preserve is a privately owned 365-acre example of land stewardship and professional game management. Whitetail deer, wild turkeys, grouse, woodcock, wood ducks, teal, mallards, and geese are the beneficiaries of studied, careful habitat management.

Brook, brown, and rainbow trout benefit as well. The two interconnected ponds have bottoms of clay, sand, silt, and limestone. Caddis, mayflies, dragonflies, damsels, leeches, and shiners provide the protein for cruising, hard-muscled trophies. Drowned trees and steep drop-offs mix with backdrops of tall hardwoods, wild flowers and grass to more open areas where casting is clear and easy. This is a good place for casting instructions and practice with privacy.

The quality of fly-fishing is, of course, the most important feature of these ponds. Throughout the day in the spring and fall, and at dawn and dusk during the summer months, the big trout cruise in search of prey. The tannic water color provides the fish a sense of security and their bulging wakes are easy to spot when they move near the surface or close to shore. From an hour or so before sunset to just after full darkness is the most productive period to fish for the larger, slab-sided rainbows. They queue up at the mouth of the inlet stream at the north end of Beaver Flats Pond and then cruise and hunt the edges past the angler's hut and the oak edges to the dam and culvert which feeds Ravine Pond. Small streamers that imitate shiners, black Woolly Buggers, Bunny Strip Leeches, and a variety of seasonal caddis and mayfly patterns—both nymph and dry—work well.

The brown trout also grow very large in this rich environment and retain the more secretive, selective, and nocturnal tendencies of their riverine brethren in this part of Michigan. In both ponds they prefer a later start to active feeding and show much more aggressive behavior on cool, overcast days. They will eat the same patterns as the rainbows but are less tolerant of sloppy casting. A Deer Hair Mouse can be effective when fished with a quick, erratic retrieve as night falls.

Big Creek Preserve's brookies are brilliantly colored with fat bodies and small heads. They have all the brilliant flash and style that endears them so, but they are not guileless. As with the browns and rainbows, careful casting with long fine leaders is more often required than not. They want specific imitative patterns fished naturally. To date, and despite considerable effort, I have been unable to hook one on a Mickey Finn, a Royal Coachman, or other patterns that we often think of as classic brook trout flies.

An angler's hut sits on the east shore of Beaver Flats Pond where the water narrows between two bowls. The hut has a tying bench and supplies, comfortable chairs, a porch with the appropriate rocking chairs and a campfire ring. It's a good place to have a cool drink and watch cruising wakes and rise forms on a summer's evening.

It is only fair to note that the fly-fishing here is much better during spring and fall then in mid-summer. A lack of rainfall (near drought conditions) has adversely affected the angling during the warmer months in 1999 and 2000. Two new larger ponds are scheduled to begin construction in the near future.

Although common enough on the east and west coasts of the United States and throughout the Rocky Mountains, "private waters" angling is in its infancy in the Great Lakes region. It is starting to gain in popularity in Michigan and it seems reasonable enough to cite one for sampling purposes.

Big Creek's owners, Steve and Deb Basl, have instituted strict rules to protect the ponds. They include: strictly no kill, barbless hooks, catch and release nets, no boats or float tubes allowed, and all anglers are cautioned to use extreme care in reviving and releasing trout. It is worth noting that injured fish are expected to be reported (strictly on the honor system) and that a $2.00-per-inch fine is levied.

Access is limited to just a few rods each day. Current conditions and reservations can be made by contacting Steve Basl, Big Creek Preserve, (989) 826-3606.

Close to the Big Creek Preserve the Au Sable River has Hexagenia limbata *hatches.*

Wakely Lake

Smaller than average for Wakely Lake.

Access to Wakely Lake's incredible fly-angling is restricted to a moderate hike along an easy trail from M-72 a few miles east of Grayling. The parking area on the north side of the highway is well marked. Wakely has no boat launch and tight angling restrictions with a limited open season. Be sure to check the regulations each year.

Approximately 100 acres in size, Wakely is a "moderate"-sized lake by Michigan's inland standards. For the last several years its fish populations have been sheltered by artificials-only and no-kill regulations along with an angling window that runs only from mid-June to the end of August. These have combined to produce extraordinary catches of large bluegills, largemouth bass, and northern pike. Most fly-anglers prefer to portage small canoes or carry in float tubes and to seek out the slab-sided bluegills and bass. An average outing on Wakely Lake for a fly-angler of moderate skill will usually produce several bluegills over 10 inches in length and bass between 15 and 18 inches.

Wakely is a shallow lake with good weed growth and submerged logs. It is fertile and produces a variety of food forms for the panfish and bass. Fish can be found just about everywhere, but most tubers and canoers follow the shoreline contour and congregate near points and small coves on the lake's west side. The north side of the lake hosts nesting loons and they must not be disturbed.

I recommend a slightly longer rod than one would use on the nearby Au Sable River. A 9 1/2-foot, 5-weight rod will give the angler a bit more backcast clearance when fishing from a canoe or sitting low to the water in a float tube. It will deliver a long line, have enough "delicacy" to enjoy the bluegills, and still provide the muscle to handle a 4-pound largemouth. Take two reels, or at least an extra spool. You will likely want to switch between a floating line and a sink-tip. Long leaders are not necessary, nor are fine tippets.

A fly selection for bluegills should include Gold Ribbed Hare's Ears, small peacock herl-bodied Woolly Buggers, damselfly nymphs, rubber-legged spiders, and panfish-sized poppers. For bass use larger poppers and Woolly Buggers and carry strip-leech patterns in yellow, olive, and black. Red-and-white, yellow-and-red, chartreuse, all-white, and all-black streamers are effective for northern pike.

Many experienced anglers regard Wakely as the finest fly-angling lake in Michigan. No doubt this is due to the restricted access, catch-and-release, and short open season limitations. Most of the angling pressure in the area is centered on the Au Sable and Manistee rivers and their glorious trout, but Wakely provides a welcome change of pace—lots of room, a quiet and lovely setting, and (probably) the largest bass and panfish in a fly-angler's career.

O'Brien Lake

This small, ultra-clear lake sits just east of the small town of McKinley very near the line between Oscoda and Alcona counties. It is easy enough to access, but first you have to find McKinley. As a starting point, take McKinley Road (just north of the bridge over the Au Sable River) east from M-33 along the north bank of the Au Sable. McKinley is 10 miles east of Mio. In McKinley you will see a small sign indicating the direction to O'Brien Lake. Follow this dirt road (keeping left) to the lake. There is a small parking area and a handicapped-accessible angling dock at the lake shore, but no boat launch. Take a small canoe or float tube for best results.

O'Brien has both rainbow and brown trout and some reach substantial proportions. They feed on a mix of small baitfish, leeches, mayflies, stoneflies, caddis, dragonfly, and damselfly nymphs.

You will often see fish cruising and gulping mayfly emergers. This exciting angling is best in May and early June during the early morning and late-evening periods. Use the same emerger patterns you would use for the Au Sable during that period. Soft-hackled emerger patterns seem to work best, but often a trailing shuck nymph pattern twitched along in the surface film is the hot ticket.

Sub-surface nymphs and streamers also work here. Fish them on a wet-tip or full-sinking line with a slow hand-twist retrieve. Gold Ribbed Hare's Ear, and Pheasant Tail Nymphs in sizes 10 to 16 are effective. Fluttering, philoplume *Hex* patterns are deadly during June and flat-bodied, dark brown (or olive) dragonfly nymphs in sizes 4 and 6 will catch fish throughout the season. You should also carry some olive damselfly nymphs and an assortment of Woolly Buggers and Marabou Leech patterns in black, olive, and brown.

I prefer a 9 1/2- or 10-foot fly-rod for lake and pond fishing. The added length helps keep my sloppy backcasts above water. Take both floating and sinking lines. For surface work, a long, fine leader is critical in O'Brien's clear water. Drop your fly several feet ahead of the cruising target and twitch the fly slightly with a soft pull on the line. If you move your fly with the rod tip, you create line slack which causes a problem in setting the hook on a quick rush and take.

The trout in this lake are well fed but not as critical and demanding as in the Au Sable, just a half mile south. Be prepared for a heavy fish, particularly at dawn and dusk. Your reel should have at least 50 yards of backing to accommodate the initial run.

Bring your camera. There are nesting bald eagles in the area along with osprey, mink, and deer. Listen for coyotes singing close by in the evening hours.

Healthy, energized rainbow trout are the main target in O'Brien Lake.

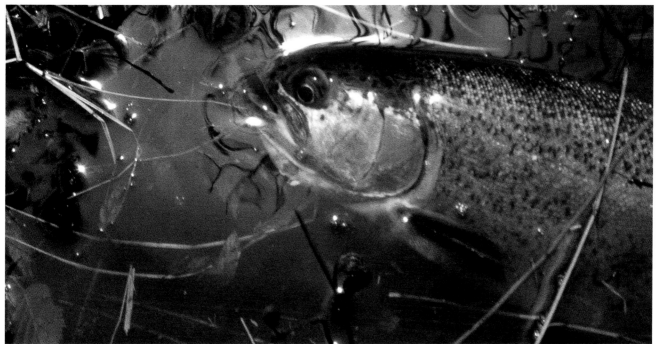

This beautiful 25-inch Au Sable brown smashed a Zoo Cougar Streamer.

Au Sable River

As a boy, I learned to fly-fish here. I grew up, went to college, grew up some more, got a job, moved away, woke up, quit my job, and moved back to the Au Sable. I will not leave. This is my home river. More accurately, it is my home; its waters both sustain and consume me. It is a wild living thing with hunters and prey on the land and in the current. Most often gentle, rarely dangerous, always seemingly indifferent, the Au Sable is one of this hemisphere's most lavish gifts. It is an *indicator* river, a significant line item on man's report card. Threats to its health point to larger problems that have a wide-ranging detrimental impact on the quality of life. If humankind can protect the Au Sable from over-use, from exploitation and greed, if we can preserve the quality of its water, lush hillsides, vigorous animal, fish, and plant life from the unrelenting crush of "progress," then our species has a chance.

The river officially begins a bit north of the town of Grayling at the confluence of Bradford and Kolka creeks. Its meander is southward to Grayling, then eastward on its push to Lake Huron. Through this course the Au Sable grows from a comfortable, gentle stream with a flow of about 75 cubic feet per second (cfs) at Grayling to over 1,400 cfs below Foote Dam. From an angler's perspective it is best to divide this considerable distance into manageable sections—each with different and significant characteristics that include, among others, size, access, and fish species.

The Au Sable is a fertile ground-spring fishery with brown trout in its headwaters and steelhead and salmon in the reach near Lake Huron.

The Holy Water (*Au Sable River*)

*A classic boat, a happy crew, and a fine day
on the "Holy Water."*

The upper part of the river is "flies-only/no kill." Its
trout have enjoyed this protection since 1988. The
Holy Water begins at Burton's Landing just east of
Grayling and continues downstream for about eight
miles to Wakely Bridge. This run of the river is
stunning and generally easy to fish. If you can picture
what a perfect small to medium-sized trout stream
would present, if you can see through its clean water
and observe the wavering grasses, the gravel, sand,
logs, and trout, if you can feel the gentle push of the
current and the sun's warmth on your face you are
seeing the Holy Water—the river of dreams.

The Holy Water supports brook, brown, and
rainbow trout along with prolific insect life,
crustaceans and forage fish. Its hatches are legendary
and the inspiration for pilgrimages of great distance.
Hendricksons, Sulphurs, mahoganies, brown drakes,
Isonychia, Tricos, caddis, stoneflies, and terrestrials
provide a taste of heaven to dry-fly enthusiasts.
Sculpins, crayfish, dace, darters, and more put some

*The traditional long and narrow Au Sable boat handles very
nicely through the tight, shallow turns of the upper river.*

Tony Petrella and Vince Edwards make final preparations for a day on the river.

The upstream view at the Whirlpool Access.

considerable heft on the trout and those that fish streamers effectively find rewards throughout the year.

Public access is generous throughout the reach. Burton's Landing, Louie's Landing, Keystone, Whirpool, Guide's Rest, Stephan Bridge, Pine Road, and Wakely Bridge are easy to find and offer fine angling. Note also that several of these are used heavily by commercial canoe liveries and it is best to explore a bit on summer weekends.

There are two fly-shops with intimate knowledge of the water. Gates' Au Sable Lodge is at Stephan Bridge. This is a full-service fly-shop with guide service and streamside rooms and restaurant. Rusty and Julie Gates own and manage this fly-angler's mecca. The Fly Factory is also on the water at the southern end of the town of Grayling. It features a wide selection of flies and equipment as well as guide service. It is owned and managed by the Southard family.

Wakely to Mio (*Au Sable River*)

A large brown trout caught at dusk near Parnalee Bridge.

Between Wakely and Parmalee bridge the river swells in size. Its width in many places is over 100 feet and the depth of its runs and pools, as well as the volume of current, become matters of consideration for wise anglers. Part of the river's growth is due to ground-spring water bubbling up from the huge aquifer, but the more significant impact is from mergers with the South Branch, the North Branch and Big Creek.

The hydraulic gradient is moderate and there is an increase of silt in this stretch of river. This combination produces ideal habitat for the world-famous *Hexagenia limbata* mayfly. The emergence usually starts around the middle of June and runs to about the 4th of July. These dates fluctuate a bit based on the severity and length of winter and early spring, but it's a safe bet that *Hex* mania will be in full swing during the third and fourth weeks of June.

Touring and local anglers are on the water before dusk and waiting for a spinner fall that usually comes during full darkness. The bugs are big, make that *really* big, and their mating swarms are often calculated to be in the tens of thousands. The subsequent spinner fall incites gluttonous feeding and the Au Sable's largest trout—fish approaching 30 inches—come to the surface. The wet, sucking plunger-like sounds of their feeding—out there somewhere in the dark—is riveting, maddening, addictive.

Rods with backbone, reels with disc drags, *careful* wading, patience, and steady nerves are helpful. If you yearn to fish the *Hex* hatch, there is no better stretch of river anywhere. Practice casting at night with big flies and stout leaders. Most often you will be casting to the sound of a rise, trying to estimate the distance out and upstream from the sound for proper placement. There is limited public access in this area. Newcomers would do well to hire a guide.

It is not only the *Hex* hatch that draws folks to this run of the Au Sable. All the major mayflies, caddis, and stoneflies are present and provide excellent angling. The same sub-surface menu items are also available to the trout. Sculpin and crayfish patterns are effective throughout the season.

The South Branch (*Au Sable River*)

Above: Chartreuse Woolly Sculpins are favorites on the South Branch.

Middle: Electro-shocking helps the fisheries biologists track survival and growth rates.

Lower: Smith Bridge on the South Branch of the Au Sable.

This major artery of the Au Sable has its own cult following. The rabid worshippers of the South Branch really don't have much, if any, need to fish elsewhere. Beginning in Lake St. Helen and flowing northward through the famous Mason Tract to its confluence with the mainstream below Wakely, the South Branch has everything a fly-rodder needs—even *wants*.

This is a gentle, smallish river but with sufficient volume and depth to hold large trout. Its hatches are abundant and reliable. Hendricksons, caddis, Sulphurs, olives, March browns, drakes, *Hex*, terrestrials, and more appear during the season. Streamers, nymphs, and wet-fly patterns are productive during non-hatch periods.

Public access is very good throughout the Mason Tract—roughly from the northern edge of the village of Roscommon to the northern boundary of the tract upstream from Smith Bridge near highway M-72.

The North Branch (*Au Sable River*)

The North Branch of the Au Sable near Lovells is both easy to wade and pleasant to fish.

This major tributary flows south through the small town of Lovells, picks up volume from Big Creek near North Down River Road, and enters the mainstream a short distance below McMasters.

The North Branch is a beginning angler's ideal classroom. It is gentle and easy to wade. It is wide enough to allow casting practice without fear of losing (too many) flies in the shoreline vegetables. It is a serene experience, generally free from canoe traffic, with good numbers of brook and brown trout eager enough to grab a fairly-cast fly.

The hatches are prolific and reliable; the access is easy, the scenery is lovely, and the trout are willing throughout its course. The Dam Four area, south of Lovells, is one of my favorite spots. It has lots of fish and is a great place to teach a newcomer to our sport.

Mio to Alcona

Bruce Chin disentangles the net from a trophy brown caught on
a streamer by brother Carl.

Left: Whitefly (Ephoron leukon) spinners below Mio.

This is "The Big Water" made famous by trophy browns and rainbows and moderate (but increasing) angling pressure. Special angling regulations have been in effect for many years on the run from Mio to McKinley, a distance of about 15 river miles, and the results are impressive. Brown trout over 20 inches are not at all rare and rainbows from 14 to 18 inches are free risers whenever there is a reasonable number of mayflies available as emergers, duns, or spinners.

It is worth mentioning that I fish this stretch most often. Over the course of nearly fifty years on this water, I have rarely seen a trout over 12 inches eat an adult caddis. This is not to say that they do not eat the nymphs, they surely do, but the adult caddis seem to go about their buggy business unthreatened by trout. Perhaps the caddis adults below Mio taste bad. I think the more likely answer is that the fish are truly spoiled and lazy. An adult caddis flutters and darts and might get away. Why waste the energy? Easier prey will be along shortly. Complementing the prolific mayfly hatches are dense populations of crayfish, sculpins, darters, dace, shiners, chubs, and juvenile trout.

The Big Water is logically divided into three sections or floats. The first run is about eight miles from the boat ramp in the town of Mio to the public access at Comins Flats off McKinley Road. This is a lovely, productive stretch of river with pools, runs, riffles, and deep holes. There are only three sites along

Cone-head streamers are effective patterns for trophy brown trout on this stretch of the river.

Right: Kelly Neuman rows while the author hangs on to a large rainbow near Comins Flats.

this course that have cabins visible from the river. The rest of the view is forest, specifically the Huron National Forest. Access is generous and easy along several USFS numbered trails on both the north and south sides of the river.

Early-season angling improves when the water temperature reaches 55 degrees F. It peaks and holds constant at temperatures between 60 and 68 degrees F. The Hendrickson hatch can be spectacular on this water when the peak emergence coincides with the magic 55-degree mark. Other hatches to note are the Sulphurs, brown drakes, *Isonychia*, and white fly.

The next downstream section is the reach from Comins Flats to McKinley. It is about the same length in terms of river miles but the river's personality changes a bit. There are more frequent stretches of slow water and there is an attendant build-up of silt. The silt, as you know by now, harbors the *Hexagenia limbata* and this adds spice to the evening soup.

Below Comins Flats there are several very deep bend holes shaded by heavy foliage. These hold super trout that will often respond to large streamers that mimic sculpins or crayfish. The riffles, particularly where they slow and blend into a pool, hold both rainbows and browns (and, rarely, brook trout) with a seeming predisposition to surface-feed. The best dry-fly action is during the Hendrickson, brown drake, and whitefly hatches, but Sulphurs and mahoganies in late May, and *Hex* during early June, can produce superb angling.

From McKinley downstream to USFS 4001, the river runs entirely through the Huron National Forest. There are no cabins or structures of any kind on this wilderness float.

The current is a bit slower and there is more silt in this reach, so the numbers of *Hexagenia limbata* mayflies increase proportionally. Usually the hatch begins about June 12 and continues through the first of July. In addition to the *Hex*, anglers find the Hendrickson, Sulphur, brown drake, *Isonychia*, and whitefly hatches rewarding. Large sculpin streamers fool big fish throughout the year, particularly at dawn or dusk, or on heavily overcast days.

Trout anglers will sometimes hook into trophy-sized smallmouth bass on streamers and, more rarely, a large walleye from one of the deep holes in this section.

Alcona to Lake Huron

There are some real trophies below the Alcona Dam.
This 25-inch brown grabbed a Zoo Cougar.

Drifting nymphs for steelhead below Foote Dam.

From Alcona to Loud Dam, the river holds a mix of rainbow trout, brown trout, smallmouth bass, and walleye. The ideal fly-rod targets are trout and bass. The trout grow large due to a combination of abundant food and very light angling pressure. The bass, likewise, put on some bulk. They are classic smallmouth—pugnacious, red-eyed scrappers. And, they are numerous. On a fair day, it is likely that a fly-angler with moderate skill will land over a dozen in the 14- to 16-inch range. Woolly Buggers, sculpins, crayfish, and rubber-legged nymphs are the favored patterns.

The riverine angling on the Au Sable picks up again below Foote Dam, the upstream barrier for salmon and steelhead from Lake Huron, a short distance west of the town of Oscoda.

From the dam, the river's flow is just a few miles to Lake Huron. The streambed is made up of sand, cobble, clay, silt, and ideal spawning gravel for salmonids. The water is crystal clear, due in part to the effect of zebra mussels and the lingering impact of several years of lower-than-normal precipitation.

Fly-anglers in pursuit of salmon and steelhead are faced with demanding conditions and the fishing is often precise in a technical sense. The clear, low water and moderate-to-high angling pressure pretty well ensures that the fish will be spooky, extremely nervous, and sensitive to anything that is unnatural.

Successful anglers fish mid-week. They use long, fine leaders and small flies. Both nymph and egg patterns need to be accurate in size and color. The best nymphs for steelhead are small *Hex* patterns, philoplume Hare's Ears, small Sparrows, green caddis, and Pheasant Tails.

The fish, both steelhead and salmon, are worth the effort. Especially the steelhead. They are in the river in fishable numbers from September through early June. And they are spectacular. I believe they are the strongest, fastest, most acrobatic of all freshwater game fish. The Au Sable steelhead seem to be more wild and frenetic than other strains in the Great Lakes basin. An October steelhead of eight pounds will likely jump five or six times and make several long, very hot runs. In the net, the look in their eyes is the essence of the word 'wild.' They are wonderful.

Throughout the Au Sable's course, public access varies. The upper river, including the North Branch and South Branch, is well represented by local maps available at the fly shops mentioned and several books, listed in the appendices, which provide additional detail.

The river from Mio to Oscoda runs largely through the Huron National Forest and accurate maps showing public access points, camping facilities, and USFS trail numbers are free at district ranger stations.

Doug Heady is pretty pleased
with this wild fall steelhead landed near the High Banks.
Right: John Van Dalen nymphing the pockets at the Boy Scout Run.

East Coast Region: Au Sable River

Hubbard Lake

Hubbard Lake's weedy shoreline is home for large northerns.

Hubbard, at nearly 9,000 acres in size, is one of Michigan's largest inland lakes. Its sheer size may be daunting at first impression, but the fact is that this lake has numerous outstanding fly-angling opportunities. It lies at the extreme northern edge of Alcona County, only a short drive inland from mighty Lake Huron. Hubbard is easily reached by well-maintained roads off US 23 to the east, M-72 to the south, and M-65 to the west.

Hubbard's shoreline is highly developed with residential homes and summer cabins. There are public launch facilities at both East Bay and North Bay. Until recently, a fee-based launch site was available at South Bay, but at this time that facility is closed.

My most recent visit to Hubbard Lake was a July outing, not usually considered a peak month for fly-angling on large, deep lakes such as Hubbard. Still, we did well. Kelly Neuman and I fished with Ed

Bolanowski, owner of East Bay Outfitters on North Hubbard Lake Road. Ed's business is not a fly-shop but rather a general tackle and outfitting supply store. There is no dedicated fly-shop in the area and Ed is the best source for current information (no nonsense, no hype) on fishing conditions.

Our first search was in the South Bay where we used Ed's boat to navigate up the West Branch River. This is a wild setting—a classic marsh plain with cattails, lily pads, and deep, clean and cool water in the river channel. Ducks, geese, heron, coots, and osprey are abundant. Muskrats and mink scurry along the edges and deer roam the hummocks. We heard loons but did not see them.

Ed navigated the boat while Kelly and I cast large streamers and poppers to the weed edges and into the lilypad tangles. The sun rose into a cloudless sky and the northerns showed but would not eat. All but one. This large pike rushed and chomped my rabbit-tailed chartreuse slider just as my attention was diverted by a flushing mallard pair. But I felt the fish and saw it. I thought there was a decent hook-set but the connection did not hold for long. The pike was in the 40-inch range. His sharp teeth severed the 30-pound mono shock-tippet with one turn of his head. "I should have used a heavier tippet." Kelly and Ed only nodded. They very decently did not pour salt on my wound.

We made a few more casts in the feeder stream, but it was clear that the pike would be tough customers until the light level faded in late evening. Ed suggested we make a run to the west shore and fish the weed beds and drop-offs in the hope that a few northerns would still be active in the bigger water of the main lake. We tried this for about an hour. Several fish followed our flies close enough to the boat so that we could clearly see them, but they would not take. With no luck, we acknowledged that the chances for a big northern were pretty well done until evening.

Ed told us that the smallmouth bass angling had been pretty good in East Bay and we made the run without delay. The water in East Bay is clear with weedbed patches and deeper open channels. We could often see bottom as we drifted in the wind and cast Clouser Minnows, crayfish patterns, and Woolly Buggers near the weed edges. We caught some beautiful smallmouth by following Ed's close directions on where to cast and how to move the fly (short strips of 10-12 inches with a distinctive pause of 2-3 seconds—this gave a definite up-and-down

Kelly casting a large streamer for pike in the outlet of West Branch River at South Bay.

This Hubbard Lake smallmouth smashed a frog-colored slider.

"hopping" motion to the fly). We used sink-tip, class IV lines on 9-foot, 8-weight rods. Kelly caught the best bass of the day, a really powerful fish that hit with a vengeance and took to the air. It just would not quit and when he finally grasped the fish by the lip and lifted it for a photo we all grinned like small boys.

It turned hot and the wind died in early afternoon. There were no clouds. Ed (knowingly) remarked that the fishing was probably through—at least for several hours—so we motored back across the big lake.

Hubbard is best fished from a motorized boat, although a float tube or canoe would be fine if you stay close to shore on a calm day. Hubbard has a wide-open expanse that can raise big waves quickly in heavy weather. A canoe would be a fine way to explore the more protected area of the West Branch River that feeds in at South Bay.

Hubbard is a great lake for fly-fishing and is under-utilized in that regard. It has large northerns, beautiful and robust smallmouth bass, and panfish. It is easily reached with good public access and has numerous motels, cabins, boat rentals, and campgrounds in the area. Be sure to check with Ed Bolanowski for an honest appraisal on the fishing. He can be reached through East Bay Outfitters at (989) 727-9916.

Klieber Pond

The public access to Klieber Pond near Onaway.

This small lake is part of the Black River system and is formed by a dam near the town of Onaway in the eastern section of Cheboygan County. This is the heart of Michigan's elk country and a visiting angler is well advised, regardless of season, to carry a camera with a telephoto lens. Some of the bulls grow magnificent antlers by late summer. As fall progresses, the leaves turn to flame, the bulls bugle and strut aggressively, and the fish in Klieber Pond are feeding heavily.

The pond has healthy populations of walleye, northern pike, and panfish. Most angling pressure is centered on the tasty walleye throughout the year. Fly-anglers who target northern pike, bluegills, and sunfish will find little competition, particularly in the spring and fall. At these times the fish are available throughout the pond and in relatively shallow water. During the heat of summer, the best fishing will be during the early-morning and late-evening hours.

There are a few cottages on the north end of Klieber and a "loose" camping area on the east side between the outlet dam and the public access and boat ramp off Twin School Road. Looking to the west from the boat launch you will see a point and a cove. Mike Moreau, the top fly-fishinging guide in the area, favors this area, and the west shoreline for northerns. Mike uses a 9-foot, 8-weight rod with a sink-tip line and

stout shock leader as a basic set-up. His favorite flies are large streamers and sliders in red and white, red and yellow, all yellow, chartreuse, and black. Some of your streamers should incorporate built-in flash in the form of Flashabou or Krystal Flash.

Fish the weed edges and deeper water just off the weeds and shoreline. We often think of northerns as always lying in ambush right at the weed edges when, in fact, they are often several feet out in deeper water.

If for some reason the fish in Klieber are not responsive, there are two more fine fly-angling ponds nearby. To the south near the Montmorency County line you will find Cornwall Pond near the intersection of Ossmun and Clark roads. There is a well-marked access trail off Ossmun which leads to a public access and launch area. Cornwall has a healthy number of aggressive tiger muskies along with bass and panfish.

A few miles to the east, across the Presque Isle County line, Tomahawk Flooding offers large pike, bass, and panfish. Tomahawk has two public access points, one on the east side and one on the west side. Both are well marked. This pond has a ragged shoreline with multiple points and coves, good weed growth, light pressure, and excellent fly-rod opportunity. It is easily approached directly off Michigan Highway 33.

IV
The Upper Peninsula

This part of the state is for more rugged explorers. There are fewer guides, outfitters, lodges, fly shops, and general human-oriented amenities. The "Upper" is true "up north", and a high percentage of it is pure wilderness. In "Michigan speak," northern Michigan is that part of the state beginning at about Clare and continuing north to the Straits of Mackinac. Upper Michigan is north of that. It has huge state and federal parks, wildlife refuges with moose and wolves, isolated wilderness research areas, a wild and stormy coast with crushing waves of water so cold that drowned boaters are preserved forever.

Exploration here is a more serious undertaking. A full tank of gas, compass, tow rope, cell phone, first-aid kit, water, blankets, maps, and jugs of mosquito repellant need to be on board your 4WD vehicle as you head out to find that isolated bass pond, those brook trout headwaters. Tell folks where you are headed, when you expect to be back. The wilderness trails are lightly traveled and maintenance is irregular. Even on the most popular trout streams, on the best isolated ponds and lakes it is possible to fish for days without seeing another person. If you want a lodge atmosphere with the company of other fly-anglers for cocktails and dinner, the UP is not for you; stick to the northern Lower Peninsula.

J.R.R. Tolkien wrote in *The Hobbit* that, "Not all who wander are lost." If you have a wanderer's soul, you will love the lonely howls of the wolves, the tremula of loons, the inspiring burst and crash of the countless waterfalls, the mesmerizing, slithering dance of the northern lights—the pure untamed wilderness of this land.

What I've written here is intended to be only a taste of the wilderness party. My book with Steve Nevala covers the trout streams in detail. Chris Deubler's book gives more direction on ponds. The vast shoreline of Superior, Michigan, and Huron are largely unexplored by fly-anglers, as is Isle Royale National Park and the countless inland lakes.

I am continually pulled north of north to the Upper Peninsula. Over the years this persistent longing has always been for the journey as well as the destination. To truly explore, to cast on remote water where the fish may have *never* seen an artificial fly is the essence of the pull of the north. For me, it would be a grievous sin to be so specific that the thrill of discovery would be lessened. If you sample what is covered here, it is a very good bet that you will be exploring the Upper Peninsula on a regular basis.

Black River Area

Guide John Ramsay led the author to this northern in the mouth of the Black River at Lake Superior.

The northwestern corner of the Upper Peninsula is one of the most sparsely populated areas of Michigan. Hard by the Wisconsin border, its few residents are more likely to cheer for the Packers and Brewers than the Lions and Tigers. Tourism and lumbering provide more jobs now than the faded mining enterprises. Within the umbrella of tourism, the dollars generated by the downhill ski industry reign supreme. Several major resorts and time-share complexes attract enthusiasts from throughout the country and just a bit north of Wakefield, the world's foremost "ski flying" hill and ramp is an awesome, spine–tingling spectacle.

Fly angling in this wild wonderland can be spectacular. The rivers and lakes are lightly fished by most national standards and the scenic grandeur is inspiring. Bordering the Lake Superior shoreline, Michigan's Porcupine Mountain State Park is a protected, rugged center for remote fly-angling adventure. Within the park's boundaries several fine trout streams (Carp, Little Carp, Presque Isle) flow north to Lake Superior. Cascading, tumbling runs blend and smooth to calm pools, then plunge again. Scenic waterfalls—some large and majestic, some small and delicate—command attention.

Outside the park, the area has many small streams that are home to truly wild native brook trout. Larger flows host trout in the upper reaches and an intriguing mix of species at or near their Lake Superior destination. Brookies are the most common and sought-after species of trout or char with rainbows a close second. Lake trout nose into the estuaries and large brown trout move seasonally to the bases of the barrier falls on most rivers. Smallmouth bass, northern pike, walleye, and carp are also present in the lower reaches.

A quick glance at a good map of the area will present a wide scope of angling opportunity, but if I had limited time, my choice would be to concentrate first on the Black River west of "the Porkies" and then on the Presque Isle on the western border of the Park.

The Black River

Above: John is hooked up to a wild brookie in a small tributary to the Black River.

Right: A living jewel—an Upper Peninsula brook trout.

This scenic wilderness river headwaters as the Little Black east of County Road 579 to the south of Wakefield. In the town of Wakefield, the Little Black enters Sunday Lake and exits as the Black River. Its flow from there is westward for a few miles to north of Bessemer, then northward to Lake Superior through a meandering, rugged ravine.

Along the way, the Black is cooled by springs and the inflow of vibrant, coldwater feeder creeks. Sapsucker, Sixmile, Powder Mill, Reed, Narrows, Kirby, Montowibo, and others nourish the larger river and provide tight-quarters fly-angling for wild brookies. The fishing is rugged and "up close" in these diminutive feeders, but the fish are eager and unsophisticated. Every spot that you think should hold a brook trout usually holds two or more. They will rush a wet or dry fly quickly if a modicum of stealth is employed. Short rods of 7 to 7 1/2 feet and a dapping technique with bright flies is the usual method. Royal Coachman wets and dries, Mickey Finn streamers, small Woolly Buggers, a few Adams dries, and a Muddler or two will be more than enough variety for these feeder-stream trout.

The fish in the Black are a different story. These brookies grow substantially larger, and in some stretches share their habitat with aggressive smallmouth bass. And the Black, by midwestern standards, is a good sized river. Longer, more powerful fly-rods are required to punch out long casts with larger flies. A 9-foot, 6-weight is a good choice because it allows both dry-fly and streamer work as required. The accesses to the Black usually involve some downhill/uphill jaunts and carrying two rods is a bit clumsy.

Favorite patterns for the Black include the selection mentioned above, as well as patterns to cover the prevailing hatch. I also carry streamers like the Zoo Cougar, Woolly Sculpin, and a dace or shiner pattern. Nymphs work well and Gold Ribbed Hare's Ears, Pheasant Tails, Woolly Worms, caddis, and stonefly patterns should also be part of your assortment.

Different sections of the river fish better than others based on flow from rain (or snow melt) and time of year. To save time, I suggest you contact John Ramsay, the top fly-fishing guide in the western U.P. John lives on the edge of the Black River gorge about two miles from Black River Harbor on Lake Superior. He is an escapee from Chicago where, several years ago, he made his living as a "blues" pianist and vocalist. The last time I visited and fished with John, his home's major furniture was a kitchen table and a piano. He's a lot of fun, knowledgeable, patient, and a sincere, dedicated advocate of coldwater conservation. He can take you to the wonders of small-stream brookies hunkered under logs in a canopied, lush wonderland, the thrill of larger trout or a wild smallmouth at the base of a thundering majestic waterfall, or the hard pull and mad dash of an enraged northern in his "tidalpool" at the Black's mouth at Lake Superior.

However you decide to explore the Black River area, be absolutely sure to bring a good camera and

This smallmouth is from the Black River upstream from Rainbow Falls.

several rolls of color film. You will see immense white pines, hemlocks, firs, and spruce the size of which are rarely seen elsewhere. The stunning waterfalls, heavy rapids, and dancing riffles set in the deep ravine will demand multiple photographs. Chippewa Falls, Algonquin Falls, Great Conglomerate Falls, Gorge Falls, Sandstone Falls, and Rainbow Falls are all worth single-purpose visits with just your camera in hand.

A Black River tributary filled with wild brookies.

Presque Isle River

Flowing near and partially through the western edge of the Porcupine Mountains Wilderness State Park, the Presque Isle always makes me think of a western foothills river. It sports Rocky Mountain type boulders, rock-strewn riffles, smooth but very quick pools, and a steeper-than-expected hydraulic gradient. It is the home of handsome rock-hard rainbow trout.

This river is born near the Wisconsin state line in the national forest lands of southern Gogebic County. It flows north through the small village of Marenisco near US Hwy. 2 and continues west of Lake Gogebic on its northward run to Lake Superior. On its way, the Presque Isle crosses MI Hwy. 28 and gathers speed and size cascading through Minnewawa, Nimikon, Nokomis, and Lepisto falls. Between Lepisto Falls and the mouth, the river runs through a series of tight turns and exuberant rapids (these rapids can turn from happy to wild and dangerous under certain conditions, use caution). All of this flow holds wild rainbow and brook trout. My better luck over the years has been with the rainbows. Although the Presque Isle has good populations of the major mayflies, caddis, and stoneflies—and therefore produces good angling during hatches and spinner falls—I've usually fared best by stripping streamers or swinging soft-hackled wets. All the sculpin patterns produce if fished with a dart-pause-dart retrieve. My favorites are the Zoo Cougar, Woolly Sculpin, and Madonna. I've always had very good results with black Woolly Buggers, cone-head Marabou Muddlers, and an old-fashioned pattern called the Pass Lake. Grouse-hackled wets with dubbed fur or peacock-herl bodies in sizes 10 to 16 are simple to fish and are very effective.

A good place to start your exploration of the Presque Isle is at the bridge on South Boundary Road within the state park. I like to walk upstream first, then fish downstream back to my car. Depending on success I'll either take a break and re–tool or continue on past the bridge and hike back upstream to the car at the close of business. A good rig to consider for your first venture is a tandem-fly set-up with a small soft-hackle wet as a dropper and a Woolly Bugger or Pass Lake as the point fly. This is a good way to probe the pockets and determine what the fish might prefer. I try to watch for "flashes" of fish turning on one fly or the

Although not common, the Presque Isle River produces some trophy rainbows.

other and adapt the rig based on what seems to be drawing the most attention.

A 9-foot, 5- or 6-weight rod is about right on this river, but I always take along a heavier rod with a full-sinking line or a fast-descent wet-tip line. If the trout in the river are sulking it's just a very short drive to the mouth at Lake Superior. Here one can find a heavy-shouldered salmon or steelhead just about any time.

Like the Black, the Presque Isle is wild, beautiful, and undeniably photogenic. Take your camera. You might see a bear, an otter, or an eagle at reasonable range.

Lower Dam Pond

Lower Dam Pond and the East Branch of the Ontonagon have both rainbow and brook trout.

This is a beautiful piece of water that sits behind a small dam on the East Branch of the Ontonagon River near the town of Kenton in southern Houghton County. Forest Highway 3500 runs right to the entrance to a small USFS campground on the pond's shore. The few campsites are nestled close to the water and a very short walk leads to the pond's outlet at a small dam on the river. I have fished Lower Dam Pond several times over the past few years and never failed to catch trout and enjoy my stay immensely.

Lower Dam Pond has both brook and rainbow trout. They tend to cruise close to the shore during early morning and evening. During two separate visits, they were actively gulping brown drake spinners. These fish were not huge but they were big enough to pull line against my drag. The rainbows I have caught in the pond have ranged from 10 to 18 inches—pretty respectable. My biggest brook trout was about 14 inches, but most were smaller. A fair guess at an average for the brook trout would be 10–11 inches. I know there

are bigger fish in the pond—I've seen them cruising in the shallows. Some of the rainbows seemed to be in the high teens, close to 20 inches.

If you camp at Lower Dam Pond or at one of the nearby campgrounds, try the outlet, the East Branch of the Ontonagon, during the day. It has both brook and rainbow trout that are (most often) quite eager to eat a fly. This is small, brush-lined water that requires a "stalk-and-dap" method in most spots. Your fly selection can be pretty basic. A few Adams, Borchers, Light Cahills, and Royal Wulffs will cover dry-fly needs. Hare's Ears, caddis, and Pheasant Tails are it for nymph patterns. The Royal Coachman streamer works in both the pond and the creek along with Woolly Buggers, small Muddlers, yellow Marabou Muddlers, and black Marabou Muddlers.

On several occasions, I've been frustrated by bigger fish sipping bugs just out of reach on the pond. A float tube or small canoe would have solved my problem, but I did not have one with me on those visits.

Lake Gogebic

Smallmouth bass are the top fly-rod species in Lake Gogebic. This one is a bit smaller than average.

This is the largest inland lake in the U.P. It is long and narrow with a prominent hook to the east (Bergland Bay) at its north end. Gogebic's 12,800 acres sit at an elevation of nearly 1,300 feet which is quite lofty by Michigan standards. The lake is a magnet for walleye anglers from throughout the Great Lakes region. Most of the attention is centered on this species but there are others, including northern pike and smallmouth bass.

Several years ago I was researching U.P. trout streams and was heading east on M-28 from the Black River near Wakefield. A local outdoors radio program caught my attention. A call-in voice was bemoaning the fact that the walleye and bass fishing had gone in the tank. The voice explained that the "mayfly hatch" was in progress on Lake Gogebic and that the fish were uncatchable until the hatch ended. The voice went on to say that the fish would only eat the "bugs" on the surface and this was particularly true along the lake's north shore in Bergland Bay.

It was late afternoon. I was entering the small town of Bergland right on Gogebic's north shore. Hmm. At a small motel on the north side of M-28, a fellow was mowing the lawn while two Labradors lounged on the porch. My lab, Cobaka, "woofed" and I pulled in the driveway. "Do you allow dogs here?" "Hell, we won't rent a room to anybody without a dog," he answered with a wide grin. He confirmed the dismal radio

fishing report. The bass and walleye just wouldn't eat anything but the big mayflies. The bass were cruising just off shore at the town park on Bergland Bay only a few blocks from his motel.

That late afternoon and early evening I watched a local softball game until about the fourth or fifth inning. The Bergland lads were trouncing the bad guys when I wandered down to the shore. Fish were gulping in the soft twilight and I was into my waders and out in the water in short order.

Hex spinners were everywhere. Struggling emergers were being eaten within 30 feet of me in a 180-degree arc. They were smallmouth bass from 12 to 16 inches and they were pushovers for the same spinner pattern that had become my favorite for the Au Sable and Manistee rivers. This is a simple fly. It has a cream or yellow foam body and palmered (and clipped short) ginger hackle. The wings are white calf tail spread in spinner fashion. The tail is moose mane with two strands of pearl Krystal Flash. The added sparkle in the tail seems to gather light and attract attention during heavy spinner falls.

Gogebic does not receive much attention from fly-anglers beyond spanking the panfish early in the season. And, to be perfectly honest, I haven't explored much of it beyond Bergland Bay. But I will. The little village of Bergland has overnight accommodations, a couple of restaurants, a nice town park, and a boat launch.

Trout Lake and West Trout Lake Pond

Upper Peninsula lakes and ponds produce some large brookies. This one was close to 20 inches long.

After buying and reading Christopher Deubler's book, *Trout Ponds and Lakes in The Upper Peninsula of Michigan,* I called the author. We talked a bit and tried to find a time to fish together but just could not manipulate our schedules enough to make it happen. I did use his book, however, to find some new water on my next visit to the U.P. West Trout Lake Pond and Trout Lake are two that I would have never found without Deubler's work.

Trout Lake, and the connected West Trout Lake Pond, is best reached via Rapid River Truck Road off M-94 south and west of Munising. The lake is long and narrow and covers about 40 acres. The pond is spring-fed and quite small at 8.5 acres. It took a little while and some hiking, sloshing, and paddling, but I managed to catch several gorgeous brookies during two successful evenings.

There were no rising fish in evidence and I had brought only one line—a floater—but it didn't seem to matter. A small split shot about 10 inches above a number-8 olive cone-head Woolly Bugger did the trick. I never changed flies on either body of water.

None of my fish were big. The heftiest was about 12-13 inches, but he was dark and wild and incredibly strong for his size. I caught several smaller, from about 8 to 11 inches, and heard a chorus of howls at dusk. Mournful and full-bodied, these wild songs were big—if a sound can be big. Coyotes are common around my home. These were not coyotes. I felt as though I had become a part of it, the *wild*.

I loved just being there.

When I go back, there will be an extra spool with a sink-tip line in my jacket. I will take small streamers, Woolly Buggers (of course), some Hare's Ears and Hex nymphs, and a handful of dry flies like the Humpy, Adams, and Royal Wulff.

St. Mary's River

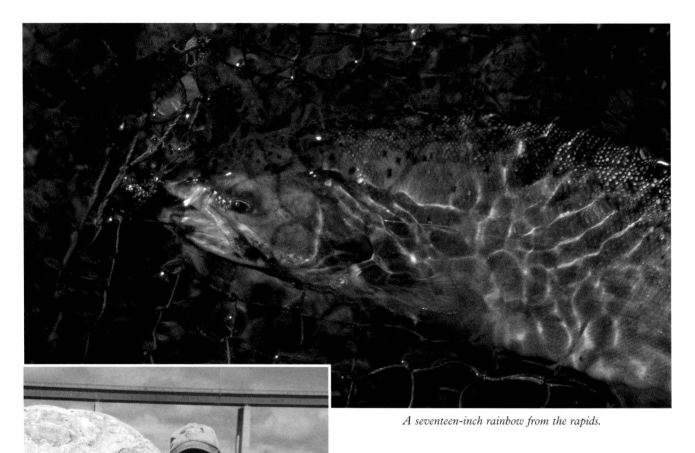

A seventeen-inch rainbow from the rapids.

Guide John Giuliani with an average-sized resident rainbow.

This is a big one. The St. Mary's drains Lake Superior into Lake Huron and creates the border of the United States and Canada at Sault Ste. Marie. The river forms at the outflow of the big lake's southeastern corner between Michigan's Upper Peninsula and Ontario. Its flow is short but impressive. On both sides of the river, huge locks raise and lower tankers, ore carriers, and other ocean vessels for their back-and-forth journeys between Lake Superior, the lower Great Lakes, and the Atlantic Ocean via the St. Lawrence.

How do you fly-fish a river over one mile wide with all the deep, churning blue of Lake Superior's icy caverns, with plowing 600-foot-long tankers, and roaring rapids that fall over 20 feet in less than a mile? *Very* carefully.

The west side of the river is American water. Its flow is deep and heavy but relatively smooth and featureless (except for those huge freighters). The Soo Edison electric generating plant sits on the shore in Sault Ste. Marie, MI. The St. Mary's current spins the turbines that power the area. Fisheries research programs are conducted within the power plant. These are directed by Roger Griel and supported by Soo Edison and Lake Superior State University as well as the cooperative participation of many others including anglers from the United States and Canada.

These research efforts have produced a viable Atlantic salmon fishery in the St. Mary's River. The Atlantics forage and grow in Lake Huron and return in classic manner to their natal water. Some ascend "the rapids" on the east side of the river in Canadian waters, but the larger percentage zero-in on the churning outflow from the turbines of the Soo Edison plant.

To say that this is a specialized form of fly-fishing is a gross understatement. Sturdy boats with stable casting platforms and reliable motors are required as a base point. Specialized "hooks" are used by guides and local anglers to attach their boats to the barrier wall of the electrical plant at the outflow tunnels for the turbines. The heavy flow pushes the boat out and away from the wall and the hook holds the boat in position. The angler looks for Atlantics holding in the current close to (sometimes tight to) the tunnel walls. The current is quick and the fish hold at a depth of several feet. They are difficult to see. The cast is made (usually) into the tunnel so that the fly (most often assisted with split shot) will tumble and drift to the proper level as it approaches the target fish. Atlantic salmon in the

St. Mary's are unbelievably snooty (from what I have read and heard, this is true of Atlantics everywhere); everything needs to be just right in order to entice a take. Small nymphs are the choice of most anglers and guides, and some of these are local patterns that are adapted slightly on a yearly basis. Standard nymph patterns that work include Hare's Ears, *Hex* nymphs, caddis, and Pheasant Tails.

A 9- or 9 1/2-foot, 7-weight rod is preferred by most. You will definitely need a quality reel with a smooth drag and lots of backing. The line is usually a "shooting" or "running" line attached to a long leader and fine tippet. The take may be subtle but the fight is not. *Salmo salar,* the leaper, lives up to its latin name in the St. Mary's. Wild jumps and blistering runs are a surety. The fish will run away from the wall and out into the huge river. The boat hook is released from the wall and you follow. With luck, the fish comes to net. You revive, release, and motor back to the wall. These Atlantics achieve some real bulk in Lake Huron. Several "line-class" records have been set in these waters, but fish in the 20-plus-pound range are very difficult to land.

A knowledgeable guide with top-notch equipment increases your odds tremendously. On the American side, it is wise to use an American guide or to be absolutely sure that your Canadian guide has the proper

Anglers line up their boats to fish nymphs to Atlantic salmon at the outflow tunnels of the Edison power plant.

permits. And, of course, the opposite is true in Canadian waters. If you fish with an experienced friend, and no payment is involved, these restrictions do not apply. Matt Supinski of Newaygo, MI guides on the American side of the St. Mary's during the peak time for Atlantics. He can be reached through the Gray Drake listing in the appendix.

The Canadian side of the river is famous for its beautiful rapids. This one-mile-long run is a rush of water so clear that it is often difficult to assess its depth. The rocks are slippery and the current is powerful. Along with the Nipigon and the Niagra, I regard the St. Mary's Rapids as the most dangerous fly-angling venue in the Great Lakes basin. Felt soles (and I suggest studs or cleats), strong legs, and extreme care are required. The rapids attract steelhead, Atlantic salmon, and Pacific salmon (pinks and chinook) in large numbers. Resident fish include rainbow trout, whitefish, and the occasional sturgeon.

The steelhead season swings into high gear in April and usually continues into early June. The fish are big—some over 15 pounds—and the heavy current gives them an advantage. You have to be very careful while following and attempting to stay close to a running fish. If you chase blindly you will find yourself in harm's way.

I prefer a 10-foot, 7-weight rod for the rapids and load the best reel I own with 150 yards of backing behind a weight-forward, clear-tip line, a long leader, and a fluorocarbon tippet. Like most places in the Great Lakes basin, a selection of basic nymphs and eggs will cover most situations. Under certain conditions the fish can be very aggressive. This is usually when a group fresh from Lake Huron holds in one of the deeper holes and pools before searching out spawning gravel. This is the time and place to swing Spey flies and sculpin patterns on a sink-tip.

Atlantic salmon begin to show in the rapids as the steelhead run tapers off in June. Because such a high percentage of the Atlantics head for the Soo Edison plant in American waters, the number of fish in the rapids are not as high as steelhead or the Pacific salmons. Still, they represent a fishable population that attracts high interest.

Hook-ups are almost always based on sight-fishing, a careful stalk, repetitive casting, and frequent fly changes. An ability to see the fish is critical and that is difficult. They appear as pale wisps of smoke (to me!) over a multi-hued rock and shale bottom. Top-quality, polarized optics are a necessity. In general, the same tackle used for steelhead is appropriate for Atlantic salmon in the rapids.

The pink-salmon run in the St. Mary's rapid is very popular with fly-anglers throughout the region.

The author mends a long line on the St. Mary's River.

Pacific salmon begin to show in the rapids during August. By September the run is in full swing with numerous chinook to 30 pounds and hordes of pinks in the two- to five-pound range. The big salmon require a 9-weight rod but catching a 3-pound pink on such an outfit is overkill. A 4- or 5-weight rig generates a lot of fun with the smaller fish, but an accidental hook-up with a 20-plus-pound chinook is a serious problem. This is the kind of problem I like to have. Carry two rods. It's easy. Stash one on the bank with your lunch and camera while you use the other.

A guide is most helpful on the rapids. Your guide will help you select the right fly and apply the right technique. More importantly, a guide will help you spot fish. Most importantly, he will keep you safe and dry. John Giuliani and Karl Vogel are two Canadian guides of high merit. I have fished with both men over the years with excellent results. They have keen eyesight, good judgment, and a thorough and up-to-the-minute knowledge of conditions. In addition to being fly-angling professionals, they are pleasant company.

Stonefly nymphs are steelhead candy.

Be sure to have the appropriate Michigan and/or Ontario fishing license for the water you intend to fish. Comfortable lodging, good restaurants, and other attractions (casinos, tours, golf) are close at hand.

Fly Patterns

The Adams is the most famous fly pattern originated in Michigan, but there are many others, less well-known yet very effective. Roberts' Yellow Drake, Borcher's Drake, Houghton Lake Special, Rusty's Spinner, and the more recent Zoo Cougar are but a few that have gained wide popularity.

Patterns developed elsewhere work just fine in Michigan's lakes and streams. Clouser Minnows, Woolly Buggers, Deceivers, Muddler Minnows, and Zonkers are popular streamers that fool trout as well as warmwater fish. Pheasant Tails, Woolly Worms, Hare's Ears, stonefly nymphs, and Sparrows produce similarly. Poppers and sliders developed by Larry Dahlberg, Dave Whitlock, and others knock the fins off bass, northerns, and panfish.

Because the state has such a wide variety of fish species and types of water, the list that follows is meant to be only a suggestion of the kinds of flies an angler should consider for both cold and warmwater angling. Be sure to carry your personal favorites; no doubt they will work just fine.

Fly Pattern Recipes

Panfish and Bass

Note: Because I buy all my poppers, sliders, rubber-legged crickets and spiders, I do not have pattern recipes for them. The rest of the bass and panfish patterns are supplied by John Vincent, Kelly Galloup, and Rock Wilson. Of special note are the Tiger Perch and Tiger Rainbow Clousers by Rock Wilson—they also work well for big trout.

Woolly Worm
Hook: TMC 2302, 6-12
Tail: Red tag, wool or hackle fibers
Body: Chenille
Hackle: Grizzly, palmered

Sparrow Nymph
Hook: TMC 2302, 8-12
Tail: Gray marabou
Body: Olive dubbing or peacock herl
Rib: Optional
Hackle: Hen pheasant or partridge
Collar: Gray philoplume

Royal Coachman, Wet
Hook: TMC 3769, 10
Tail: Brown hackle
Butt: Peacock herl or chartreuse dubbing
Wing: Optional; white duck wing
Hackle: Brown hen

Tiger Perch Clouser
Eyes: Dumbbell
Hook: Tiemco 411S, 2-6
Wing: Yellow bucktail, orange bucktail, green Krystal Flash, green bucktail barred with Black Prismatic Marker
Throat: Red marabou

Tiger Rainbow Clouser
Hook: Tiemco 411S, 2-6
Belly: White bucktail, pearl Flashabou
Wing: Pink bucktail, light blue bucktail

Mann's Bottle Brush
Hook: Tiemco 5263, 8
Tail: Rubber legs
Body: Palmered hackle
Head: Bead head or cone head
Antennae: Rubber, various colors

Girdle Bug
Hook: TMC 5262, 8
Tail: Rubber Sili-Legs, white
Body: Chenille
Legs: Rubber Sili-Legs
Body color: Can vary
Rubber legs: Various colors

Frog Diver
Hook: TMC 8089, 2-6
Thread: 3/0 plus snag guard wire
Tail: Natural grizzly, olive & dark grizzly
Collar: White deer, topped with yellow, black and olive deer
Head: White deer, topped with yellow, black deer
Legs: Yellow rubber
Eyes: Doll eyes

Near 'Nuff Sculpin, Olive
Hook: TMC 5263, 4-10
Thread: 6/0
Eyes: Lead, painted
Tail: Olive grizzly hen hackles
Rib: Olive thread
Head: Same as body
Hackle: Olive grizzly, soft, palmered

Bead Head Rubber Leg Squirrel
Hook: TMC 5262, 6-12
Thread: Brown
Tag: Pearlescent flat tinsel
Tail: Fox squirrel tail
Rib: Same as tag
Abdomen: Squirrel dubbing
Legs: Green rubber
Thorax: Black Angora
Collar: Saddle hackle

Gobie Bugger
Hook: TMC 300, 4-8
Thread: UNI-Thread 6/0
Body: Olive marabou
Tail: Olive
Head: Olive chenille over dumbbell eyes
Fins: Partridge, olive

Bass & Panfish

Black Woolly Worm Yellow Woolly Worm Mannis Bottle Brush Near Nuff Sculpin

Olive Girdle Bug Black Girdle Bug Bead Head Rubber-legged Squirrel Gobie Bugger

Clay's Ultra Clouser Clouser Minnow

Tiger Perch Clouser Frog Diver

Green Rubber-legged Popper Red Rubber-legged Popper Black Rubber-legged Popper

Green Rubber Spider Yellow Rubber Spider White Panfish Popper Green Panfish Popper

Selected Trout Flies

Gold Ribbed
Hare's Ear

Bead Head
Pheasant Tail

Little Black
Stone

Hex Nymph

Caddis Nymph

Galloup's
Crippled Spinner

Adams
Parachute

Thorax
Hendrickson

Roberts
Yellow Drake

White Fly

Hair Wing
Caddis

Brown Drake Parachute

Foam Hex Emerger

Krystal Hex

Woolly Bugger

White Zonker

Rattlesnake

Madonna

Zoo Cougar

Cone-head Marabou Muddler

Woolly Sculpin

Woolhead Sculpin

Trick or Treat

Clay's Ultra Clouser
Hook: TMC 811S, 2/0-8
Thread: Mono thread
Eyes: Painted dumbbell eyes
Tail: Super Hair, gray and UV Flash
Wing: Super Hair, gray

Clouser Minnow
Hook: TMC 811S, size 2/0, 2 & 6
Thread: Chartreuse
Eye: Painted dumbbells
Tail: Chartreuse bucktail
Wing: White bucktail with Pearl Krystal Flash

Selected Trout Flies

Flies and recipes in this group were supplied by Kelly Neuman, Kelly Galloup, Ray Schmidt, and the author. Ray's streamers, Madonna and Rattlesnake, Galloup's Zoo Cougar and Woolly Sculpin, and the author's Trick or Treat are exceptional big trout patterns.

Nymphs

Hex Nymph
Hook: TMC 5263, 2/0-6
Dressing: Same as East Coast Steelhead except hook
Eyes: Mono or plastic bead-chain eyes, optional

Gold Ribbed Hare's Ear
Hook: TMC 5262 or Orvis 1524, 10-18
Tail: Hare's mask guard hairs
Body: Hare's ear blend dubbing, picked out
Rib: Fine gold wire
Wing case: Optional; peacock herl, or goose/duck wing fibers

Pheasant Tail
Hook: TMC 5262 or Orvis 1524, 12-20
Tail: Pheasant tail fibers
Abdomen: Pheasant tail fibers
Rib: Fine copper wire
Thorax: Peacock herl
Wing case: Pheasant tail fibers
Legs: Pheasant tail fibers
Bead Head: Optional; copper or gold

Little Black Stone
Hook: TMC 3761 or Orvis 1641, 12-16
Tail: Black goose biots

Thorax: Black dubbing mix
Wing case: Black Swiss straw

Caddis Soft Hackle
Hook: TMC 3761 or Orvis 1641, 12-18
Tail: None
Body: Squirrel blend dubbing, color of choice
Rib: Optional; fine gold wire
Hackle: Hungarian partridge
Head: Peacock herl

Dry Flies

Galloup's Crippled Spinner
Hook: TMC Galloup's Cripple, 12-20
Tail: Hackle fibers
Body: Super Fine dubbing, color to match natural
Wing: Z-lon (one)
Thorax: Super Fine dubbing to match abdomen
Hackle: Dyed grizzly to match abdomen

Adams Parachute
Hook: TMC 100, 10-18
Tail: Ultra-fine deer hair
Body: Adams blend (gray) dubbing
Post/Wing: Fine calf tail
Hackle: Brown and grizzly mixed

Thorax Hendrickson
Hook: TMC 100, 12-14
Tail: Dun hackle fibers
Body: Pinkish-gray dubbing
Wing: Fine calf tail
Hackle: Dun

Parachute White Fly
Hook: TMC 5212, 12-16
Tail: White hackle fibers
Body: White dubbing or white foam
Wing: White calf tail or fine deer hair
Hackle: White

Roberts Yellow Drake
Hook: Orvis 1523 or TMC 100, 10-20
Tail: Pheasant tail fibers
Body: Pale, fine deer hair
Wing: Fine white calf tail or deer hair
Hackle: Brown or ginger
Note: Yellow thread is important for this pattern

Hairwing Caddis
Hook: TMC 100, 10-18
Body: Dubbing, color of choice

Hackle: Palmered, color to complement body
Wing: Deer or elk hair

Bob's Krystal Hex
Hook: TMC 5212, TMC 200R or Orvis 1638, 6-8
Tail: Moose mane with two strands of pearl Krystal Flash
Body: Yellow foam
Hackle: Ginger, palmered
Wings: Calf tail or white deer hair

Foam Hex Emerger
Hook: TMC 200R, 6-8
Tail: Two strands of pearl Krystal Flash
Abdomen: Brown foam
Wing: Deer or elk hair
Thorax: Cream dubbing
Hackle: Brown
Eyes: Optional; small plastic bead chain

Brown Drake/Isonychia Parachute
Hook: Orvis 1523, TMC 5212, 10
Tail: Moose mane
Wing: White deer hair
Hackle: Brown drake: brown; for *Isonychia*: dun
Thread: For brown drake: yellow; for *Isonychia*: maroon

Streamers

Conehead Marabou Muddler
Hook: TMC 300 2-8
Thread: 3/0
Tail: Red hackle fibers
Body: Gold Mylar tinsel
Wing: Yellow, white, black, cream, olive, or chartreuse marabou
Throat: Red hackle fibers
Head: Natural deer body hair and gold cone

Madonna
Hook: TMC 300, 2-8
Thread: Danville Super Strong to match head
Body: Gold or silver Mylar tinsel
Underwing: Pearl Flashabou
Collar: Deer body hair
Head: Deer body hair, clipped

Rattlesnake
Stinger hook: TMC 2457, 10
Body hook: TMC 105, size 6
Thread: Danville Super Strong to match head

Body: Five 1/8-inch beads
Wing: Rabbit strip
Collar: Natural deer hair
Head: Natural deer hair

Wool Head Sculpin

Hook: TMC 300, 4
Thread: 3/0 olive
Tail: Olive 1/8-inch rabbit strip
Body: Olive 1/8-inch rabbit strip
  wound around hook and clipped
  on bottom
Pectoral fins: Olive hen saddle
Head: Olive wool, spun and clipped

White Zonker

Hook: TMC 300, 2-8 weight
Thread: White 3/0
Underbody: Pearl Mylar
Wing: White rabbit strip
Overwing: Pearl Flashabou
Throat: White rabbit
Eyes: Yellow and black painted

Zoo Cougar

Hook: TMC 300, 2 or 4
Thread: Danville Super Strong, color to
  match head
Tail: Yellow Marabou
Body: Pearl Sparkle braid
Wing: Mallard flank feather dyed wood-
  duck yellow
Underwing: White calf tail
Collar: Olive-yellow deer hair
Head: Olive-yellow deer hair, clipped
  and trimmed

Woolly Sculpin

Hook: TMC 300, 2-6
Thread: Danville Super Strong, color to
  match head
Tail: Marabou, color to match body
Rib: Palmered hackle, color to match
  body
Collar: Deer body hair, color to match
  body
Head: Deer body hair, clipped and
  trimmed, color to match body

Woolly Bugger

Hook: TMC 300, 2-10
Thread: 3/0 to match body
Tail: Marabou, color to match body
Body: Medium chenille, color of choice
Rib: Saddle hackle palmered to head,
  color to match

Trick or Treat

Hook: TMC 300, 2-6
Thread: 3/0
Tail: Brown, olive, tan grizzly marabou
  (mixed), four strands of Krystal Flash,
  two pumpkin-colored Sili-Legs
Body: Medium tan chenille or sparkle
  chenille
Rib: Palmered brown hackle
Wing: Mixed grizzly marabou to match
  tail
Legs: Pumpkin Sili-Legs
Head: Black or gold cone

Selected Steelhead Flies

Author's note: The differences in water color (or tint), flow, clarity, and degree of fertility between East and West Coast rivers in Michigan are slight but real. Over time, astute anglers and guides have developed very specific patterns that work best on their local rivers. Examples of this can be seen in the subtle distinctions between the flies represented here. Thanks to Ray Schmidt for tying the West Coast flies and to Kelly Neuman for the East Coast patterns. Note the different Hex nymphs for the Manistee and Au Sable.

West Coast

Autumn Spey

Thread: Bright red or cherry 3/0
  monocord or single-strand floss
Hook: TMC 7999 sized to your liking,
  I prefer 1/0
Body: 1 orange, 1 cherry red marabou
  plume, barbells stripped off one side.
  Start with the orange at the halfway
  point on the hook shank. Palmer
  forward. Tie in the cherry red at the
  orange end point and palmer
  forward
Flash: 4 red and 2 purple strands of
  Flashabou, tied on top, cut off the
  same length as the marabou
Collar: 1 purple marabou, stripped and
  wound at head
Head: Bright red
Suggestion: Tie all marabou in by the tip
  of the feather

Purple Snow Spey

Thread: Same as above
Hook: Same as above
Body: White marabou tied as above
Flash: 4 strands white and 2 strands of
  purple Flashabou
Collar: Purple marabou as above
Head: As above

Chartreuse Kingfisher Spey

Thread: Same as above
Hook: Same as above
Body: Chartreuse marabou tied as above
Flash: 4 strands pearl and 2 strands red
  Flashabou
Collar: Kingfisher blue marabou or
  schlappen
Head: As above

Dark Water Spey

Thread: Same as above
Hook: Same as above
Body: Red marabou, purple marabou
  tied as autumn Spey above
Collar: Black marabou as above
Head: As above

Orange and Red Spey

Thread: Same as above
Hook: Same as above
Body: Orange marabou tied as above
Flash: 6 strands of red Flashabou
Collar: Red marabou as above
Head: As above

Steelhead Woolly Bugger

Hook: Tiemco # 3761 or Daiichi
  #1530, 6
Thread: 3/0 waxed monocord (black)
Tail: Black marabou with peacock
  Krystal Flash
Rib: Copper wire (optional)
Body: Peacock herl
Hackle: Furnace saddle hackle

P.M. Stone

Hook: Tiemco #2457, 6 or Daiichi
  #1530, 6
Thread: 3/0 waxed monocord (dark
  brown)
Tail: Pheasant tail central fibers
Shell back: Pheasant tail central fibers
Rib: Fine copper wire
Body: Peacock herl
Legs: Pheasant tail central fiber butts

Selected Steelhead Flies
East Coast Flies

Black Stone

Pheasant Tail

Hare's Ear

Hex Nymph

Sparrow Nymph

Bright Green Caddis

Latex Wiggler

Nuke Egg

West Coast Flies

PCP
Pheasant Tail

Stone

Schmidt's Hex

Antron Bug

Caddis

Steelhead Bugger

Orange Marabou Spey

Green Marabou Spey

Purple Marabou Spey

Flats Flies

Diamond Joe

Half & Half Bendback

Go 110

Ultra Clouser

Buzz Lyte Year

Jamie's Crazy Carper

Multi-colored Diver

Hedgehog

Rabbit Strip Diver

Lefty's Deceiver

Fire Tiger

Howard Johnson's

Berry's Pike Fly

Conomo Special

Foxzilla

Schmidt's Hex Nymph

Hook: Tiemco 200R or Partridge CS54, (weighted)
Thread: 3/0 light orange
Eyes: Burned black mono
Tail: Pheasant tail central fibers
Shell back: Pheasant tail central fibers
Rib: Fine copper wire
Body: Golden stone Awesome 'Possum w/20 percent Hex Antron dubbing blended in
Wing case: Pheasant tail central fibers (treated with Flex-seal or Flexament)
Thorax: Same as body
Legs: Partridge or hen saddle

Antron Bug

Hook: Tiemco #9395 or Tiemco #3761, 6
Thread: 3/0 waxed monocord to match body color
Eyes: 3 mm black plastic bead chain
Tail: Antron yarn, dark brown for stone and *Hex*; cream for shrimp (white)
Hackle: Furnace saddle hackle for stone and *Hex*; ginger for shrimp (white)
Body: Medium chenille, black for stone, tan for *Hex*, white for shrimp (white)
Shell back: Same as tail

Schmidt's Caddis Larva

Hook: Tiemco #2457, 8
Thread: 3/0 waxed monocord (black)
Rib: Gold or copper Krystal Flash
Body: Micro chenille colors to simulate larva; caddis green, chartreuse, olive, etc.
Thorax: Peacock herl

PCP Nymph
(Pheasant, Copper, Peacock)

Hook: Tiemco #2457, 8-10
Thread: 3/0 waxed monocord (dark brown)
Tail: Ring-necked pheasant tail central fibers
Rib: Fine copper wire
Body: Ring-necked pheasant tail central fibers
Thorax: Peacock herl
Wing Case: Ring-necked pheasant tail central fibers

East Coast

Bright Green Caddis

Hook: TMC 2457, 8-10
Thread: Black
Body: Vinyl rib
Hackle: Soft partridge
Head: Peacock herl

Hex Nymph

Hook: TMC 200, 8
Thread: Brown
Tail: Partridge philoplume
Back: Pheasant tail
Rib: Fine gold wire
Body: Yellow-brown dubbing
Eyes: Small mono eyes
Hackle: Partridge philoplume

Pheasant Tail

Hook: TMC 3769, 8-10
Thread: Brown
Tail: Pheasant tail fibers
Body: Pheasant tail fibers wrapped
Wing case: Pheasant tail
Thorax: Peacock herl or dubbing
Hackle: Pheasant

Black Stone

Hook: TMC 3761, 8-10
Thread: Black
Tail: Black goose biots
Body: Dubbing black
Rib: Vinyl rib black small
Wing case: Turkey tail
Hackle: Pheasant black

Latex Wiggler

Hook: Mustad 37160, 8
Thread: Brown
Body: 1/4-inch strip latex, wrapped
Hackle: Ginger saddle
Tail: Squirrel tail
Back: Colored with Pantone pen covered with head cement

Sparrow

Hook: TMC 3761, 8
Thread: Olive
Body: Olive dubbing
Tail: Pheasant philoplume
Hackle: Pheasant rump and philoplume

Hare's Ear

Hook: TMC 3761, 8-10
Thread: Black
Body: Light hare's ear dubbing
Rib: Gold wire
Wing case: Peacock herl
Eyes: Small mono eyes
Hackle: Soft partridge

Nuke Egg

Hook: TMC 105, 8-10
Inner egg: Dark shade of red or orange McFlyfoam yarn
Outer yarn: Lighter shade, Oregon Cheese or egg, Glo Bug yarn

Flats Flies

Thanks to John Vincent of the Fly Mart in Royal Oak for the Jamie's Crazy Carper pattern, and to Russ Maddin of The Troutsman in Traverse City for the rest of the flies in this category.

Jamie's Crazy Carper

Hook: Dai-Riki 930, 6-8
Body: Ultra chenille
Wing: Mink or rabbit strip with root beer Krystal Flash

Ultra Hair Clouser

Hook: Mustad 3497, 2/0-8
Wing: Tan Ultra hair layered with white, 8 to 12 strands of Holographic Flashabou
Eyes: Hourglass
Thread: mono

Go 110

Hook: Mustad 34011, 2/0-1
Wing: Black 3/0 bucktail layered color of choice with intermittent Flashabou
Overwing: Peacock
Eyes: Bead chain, black

Buzz Lyte Year

Hook: Mustad 34011 or TMC 9394–2
Wing: Bozo Hair: Layers: black, chartreuse, pink, gray, glow-in-the-dark Flashabou, white, pink, chartreuse
Thread: Mono

Diamond Joe

Eyes: Deep Sea eyes, holographic center to match
Hook: Mustad 3407, 2/0-4
Collar: Gray schlappen
Tail: Bozo Hair two tone or color choice (chartreuse-white, black-white, white-blue) with intermittent Flashabou
Note: Use a mono loop on rear of hook to prevent rolling.

Half & Half
(Half Clouser, Half Deceiver)

Hook: 3407, 2/0-4
Thread: 3/0 matching colors
Tail: Chemise saddles, Flashabou
Eyes: Deep Sea Eyes
Note: Front of fly tied as Clouser in desired colors

Bend Back
Sparse pattern of layered bucktail with Flashabou tied in front of hook
Hook: Mustad 34005, 1/0
Overwing: Peacock

Musky and Northern Pike Flies

Thanks to Kelly Galloup and Rock Wilson of The Troutsman and John Vincent of Fly Mart for supplying these patterns and recipes.

Conomo Special
Hook: TMC 300 saltwater, 2-8
Thread: 3/0 white
Body: White Bug Fly fiber, pearl Krystal Flash
Wing: Red bucktail top, white bucktail bottom
Throat: Red Flashabou
Eyes: Painted yellow and black

Berry Pike Fly
Hook: 1/0 saltwater hook
Body: Chartreuse rabbit
Tail: Chartreuse rabbit and Krystal Flash

Rabbit Strip Diver
Hook: TMC 8115, 1-4
Thread: 3/0 olive
Guard: Wire
Tail: Olive rabbit strip
Body: Olive rabbit strip
Collar: Olive deer trimmed on bottom
Head: Olive deer

Foxzilla
Hook: Mustad 34001, #2/0
Head: Weed guard, white Estaz
Collar: Silver fox fur strip
Tail: White Bozo Hair with black felt marker barbs over Flashabou over gray Bozo Hair

Michigan's McKenzie Foundation raises money within the fishing industry for children with special needs. Call (800) 308-7688 to contribute.

Fire Tiger
Hook: Tiemco 9394 nickel
Head: Gold Estaz
Collar: Yellow schlappen over orange schlappen
Tail: Yellow Bozo Hair on bottom under orange Bozo Hair under green Flashabou under green Bozo Hair with black barbs made with waterproof marker

Multi-Color Diver
Hook: Tiemco 8089 NP, 2
Tail: Yellow Icelandic sheep orange 6 strands gold Flashabou
Abdomen: White crosscut bunny strip
Collar: Green deer hair
Head: White and green deer hair

Hedgehog
Hook: Tiemco 8089 NP, 2
Tail: Steamer hackle
Body: Stacked hair
Note: Trim bottom flat

Howard Johnson's
Hook: Mustad 34001, 1/0
This fly is layered using Icelandic sheep hair
1. Yellow hair on bottom topped with 12 stands of bullfrog Flashabou
2. Orange sheep hair topped with olive sheep hair
3. Prismatic eye then dipped in Softex

Super Hatches for Michigan Trout Streams

Hatch	Period	Size
Mayflies		
Blue-Winged Olive (*Baetis vagans*)	late April through May	18-20
Mahogany (*Paraleptophlebia adoptiva*)	May	16
Hendrickson (*Ephemerella subvaria*)	late April, May	12-14
Sulphur (*Ephemerella invaria*)	late May	14
Sulphur (*Ephemerella dorothea*)	late May–early June	16-18
Gray Drake (*Siphlonurus rapidus*)	late May–early June	12
Brown Drake (*Ephemera simulans*)	early June	10
Hex (*Hexagenia limbata*)	mid to late June	6
Light Cahill (*Stenacron*)	July and August	12-14
Blue-Winged Olive (*Ephemera lata*)	July and August	16
Trico (*Tricorythodes stygiatus*)	August, early September	24
White Fly (*Ephoron leukon*)	mid August–September	14
Caddis		
Little Black Caddis (*Chimarra aterrima*)	late April, early May	18
Popcorn Caddis (*Nectopsyche*)	June, July	14-16
Rusty Caddis (*Ptilostomis*)	June, July	8-10
Gray Caddis (*Brachycentridae*)	May, June	14
Brown Caddis (*Pycropsyche*)	August, September	10-12
Stoneflies		
Giant Black (*Pteronarcys dorsata*)	June, July	4
Brown Stonefly (*Isoperla signata*)	May	10
Yellow Sally (*Isoperla biliniata*)	June, July	14

Appendix B
Fly Shops, Outfitters, Guides

Michigan has many professionally-staffed fly-shops as well as first-class outfitters and guides located throughout the major metropolitan regions and the "destination" areas. Those listed below are truly service-minded and have been most helpful to me over the years.

Metro Detroit

Fly Mart
1002 N. Main St.
Royal Oak, MI 48067
(248) 584-2848

Angler's Den
8185 Holly Road
Grand Blanc, MI 48439
(810) 953-5530

South Branch Supply
203 East University
Rochester, MI 48307
(248) 650-0440

McGregor's Outdoors
803 N. Main St.
Ann Arbor, MI 48104
(734) 761-9200

Bueter's Outdoors
120 East Main St.
Northville, MI 48167
(248) 349-3677

Lansing Area

M. Chance Fly Fishing
5100 Marsh Rd.
Okemos, MI 48864
(877) 359-8937

Midland, Bay City, Saginaw

Little Forks Outfitters
143 E. Main
Midland, MI 48640
(877) 550-4668

Country Anglers, Jac Ford
2080 So. Thomas Rd.
Saginaw, MI 48609
(989) 781-0997

Grand Rapids

Thornapple Outfitters
1200 East Paris
Grand Rapids, MI 49546
(616) 975-3800

Great Lakes Fly Fishing Co.
2775 10 Mile Rd.
Rockford, MI 49341
(800) 303-0567

Northwest Michigan

The Gray Drake (Matt Supinski)
7616 So. Hazelwood
Newaygo, MI 49337
(231) 652-2868

Pere Marquette River Lodge
Rte. 1, Box 1290
Baldwin, MI 49304
(231) 745-3972

John Hunter
1193 Plains Rd.
Leslie, MI 49251
(517) 589-9401

John Kluesing
1141 Wolf Lake Drive
Baldwin, MI 49304
(231) 745-3792

Schmidt Outfitters
P.O. Box 211
Wellston, MI 48689
(888) 221-9056

The Troutsman
4386-A US 31 North
Traverse City, MI 49686
(800) 308-7688

Bob Clark
4585 Schoedel Rd.
Manistee, MI 49660
(231) 889-3529

Streamside Outfitters
4400 Grand Traverse Village
Williamsburg, MI 49690
(231) 938-5337

Northeast Michigan

Gates Au Sable Lodge
417 Stephan Bridge Rd.
Grayling, MI 49738
(989) 348-8462

The Fly Factory
P.O. Box 709
Grayling, MI 49738
(989) 348-5844

Bachelder Spool & Fly
South M-33
Rose City, MI 48671
(989) 685-8811

Kelly Neuman
Streamside
2085 N. Abbe
Fairview, MI 48621
(989) 848-5983

Fuller's North Branch Outing Club
6122 East Cty. Rd. 612
Lovells, MI 49738
(989) 348-7951

Mike Moreau
North-East Fly Fishing
19114 Co. Rd. 638
Onaway, MI 49765
(989) 733-6050

Upper Peninsula

John Ramsay
N15414 Black River Rd.
Ironwood, MI 49938
(906) 932-4038

The Bow Doctor
100 W. Cloverland
Ironwood, MI 49938
(906) 932-5253

St. Mary's River (Canada)

John Guiliani
Northern Fishing Adventures
553 Queen St. West
Sault Ste. Marie, Ontario P6A 1A8
(705) 942-5473

Karl Vogel
RR #2
Goulais River, Ontario P05 1E0
(705) 649-3313

Appendix C
Suggested Reading

C. Deubler: *Trout Ponds and Lakes in The Upper Peninsula of Michigan*, Siskiwit Press

B. Linsenman & S. Nevala: *Trout Streams of Michigan*, second edition, Countryman Press

B. Linsenman & S. Nevala: *Great Lakes Steelhead*, Countryman Press

B. Linsenman: *River Journal: The Au Sable River*, Frank Amato Publications

K. Galloup: *Cripples and Spinners*, Dean Publishing

M. Supinski: *River Journal: Pere Marquette*, Frank Amato Publications

M. Supinski: *Steelhead Dreams: The Theory, Method, Science and Madness*, Frank Amato Publications

R. Kustich & J. Kustich: *Fly Fishing for Great Lakes Steelhead*, West River Publishing

T. Huggler: Fish Michigan: *100 Southern Michigan Lakes*, Friede Publications

T. Huggler: Fish Michigan: *100 Northern Michigan Lakes*, Friede Publications

Fisheries Division: *Michigan's Blue Ribbon Trout Streams*, Michigan Department of Natural Resources

Michigan Atlas & Gazetteer, DeLorme Mapping

Appendix D
Information Sources

Institute for Fisheries Research
MDNR
212 Museums Annex Bldg.
Ann Arbor, MI 48109
(734) 663-3554

Michigan Department of Natural Resources
P.O. Box 30028
Lansing, MI 48909
(517) 373-1280
(www.dnr.state.mi.us)

Fishing HOTLINE (800) ASK FISH
Violations   (800) 292-7800
Weekly Fishing Reports
                    (517) 373-0908
Wildlife Div.   (517) 373-1263
Hearing Impaired   (517) 373-1137
Travel Michigan   (517) 373-0670
Law Division   (517) 373-1230

Lake Superior Management Unit
Rte. 4, Box 796
Newberry, MI 49868
(906) 293-5131

Northern Lake Michigan Management Unit
1420 US 2 West
Crystal Falls, MI 49920
(906) 875-6622

Central Lake Michigan Management Unit
8015 Mackinaw Trail
Cadillac, MI 49601
(231) 775-9727

Southern Lake Michigan Management Unit
621 N. 10th St.
Box 355
Plainwell, MI 49080
(616) 685-6851

Northern Lake Huron Management Unit
1732 M-32 West
Gaylord, MI 49735
(989) 732-3541

Southern Lake Huron Management Unit
503 N. Euclid Ave.
Bay City, MI 48706
(989) 684-9141

Lake Erie Management Unit
38980 Seven Mile Rd.
Livonia, MI 48152
(734) 953-0241

Selected Parks
West Coast Region

Burt Lake Park: at Indian River, camping, excellent fishing for northern pike.

Fisherman's Island State Park: on Lake Michigan beach near Charlevoix, camping, fishing.

Leelanau State Park: north of Northport on Leelanau Peninsula, camping, fishing on Grand Traverse Bay and Lake Michigan.

Newaygo State Park: on Hardy Dam Pond near Newaygo, camping, fishing on pond and Muskegon River.

Orchard Beach State Park: at Manistee, camping, fishing, Manistee River.

Petoskey State Park: Petoskey on Grand Traverse Bay, camping, fishing.

Sleeping Bear Dunes National Lake Shore: Empire, camping, fishing.

East Coast Region

Aloha State Park: on Mullet Lake south of Cheboygan, campsites, boat launch.

Clear Lake State Park: north of Atlanta, camping, fishing and close to Black, Sturgeon and Pigeon Rivers.

Hartwick Pines State Park: Grayling, camping, fishing on nearby Au Sable River, virgin white pines.

Rifle River Recreation Area: Lupton, camping, fishing on lakes, Rifle River and tributary streams.

Island Lake USFS Campground: north of Rose City, camping, fishing.

Upper Peninsula

Baraga State Park: south of Baraga close to Keweenaw Bay, camping, boating, fishing.

Bewabic State Park: west of Crystal Falls, campsites, fishing.

Brimley State Park: on Whitefish Bay, campsites, fishing.

Isle Royale National Park: wilderness island in Lake Superior, camping, fishing for brook trout.

Lake Gogebic State Park: western UP, camping, fishing, waterfalls.

Porcupine Mountains State Park: east of Ironwood, wilderness, camping, hiking, Lake Superior shoreline, fishing at Black River, Presque Isle River and more.

Tahquamenon Falls State Park: southwest of Watersmeet, camping, fishing, wilderness exploration.

More Helpful Books for Midwest Fly-Fishing

ONTARIO AND WISCONSIN BLUE-RIBBON

FLY-FISHING GUIDE

Spectacular photography and in-depth local knowledge highlight these useful fly-fishing guides; many fly-fishers are enjoying the enormously popular "Blue-Ribbon Fly Fishing Guide" series. Each full-color book is filled with information on the flyfishing in a particular state, including: successful techniques; productive flies and their patterns; hatch information; reading water; fish species; conservation issues; fly plates; local resources; map; and so much more. Useful and attractive, these guides are perfect for both visiting and local anglers. 8 1/2 x 11; Full color; 80 to 100 pages. **$24.95 each**

ONTARIO
Scott Smith
SB: $24.95   ISBN: 1-57188-162-X

WISCONSIN
By R. Chris Halla
SB: $24.95   ISBN: 1-57188-161-1

DRIFTBOATS
A Complete guide
Dan Alsup

Driftboats have a long, and at times controversial, history in their native Oregon. Commonplace on Pacific Northwest waters, the popularity of driftboats is enjoying a surge eastward and today are found in every state. Now comes a comprehensive guide to driftboats, this book covers: the history; the controversy; contemporary boats; purchasing and outfitting a driftboat; rowing basics; reading water; drifting a river; solutions to common river problems; checklists; the future of driftboating; and more. Written with safety and courtesy at the forefront, this guide has all the information you need to be a responsible boat owner and operator. 8 1/2 x 11 inches, 95 pages.
SB: $19.95   ISBN: 1-57188-189-1

READING WATER
Darrell Mulch

Understanding water currents and how different flies react to them is at the heart of fly fishing. In this very thoughtful book, Darrell Mulch presents his ideas concerning fly types and water dynamics and how you should approach the stream. His drawings are extremely helpful for anglers wanting to know more about recognizing and approaching the different lies fish prefer. 8 1/2 x 11 inches, 64 pages all-color.
SB: $15.00   ISBN: 1-57188-256-1

MATCHING MAYFLIES
Everything You Need to Know to Match Any Mayfly You'll Ever Encounter
Dave Hughes

Mayflies are the most important order of aquatic insects to those who fly fish for trout. In order to fish their hatches successfully, it is essential to understand their four important stages—nymphs, emergers, duns, and spinners—and to carry and know when to use the best fly patterns for each phase of this life cycle.

Dave has been studying mayfly hatches, photographing them, tying flies to match them, and honing presentation techniques to fish those flies for more than 30 years. Now you can benefit from Dave's vast on-stream knowledge.
Full-color, 8 1/2 x 11 inches, 84 pages.
SB: $25.00   ISBN: 1-57188-260-X
SPIRAL HB: $39.95   ISBN: 1-57188-261-8

FEDERATION OF FLY FISHERS FLY PATTERN ENCYCLOPEDIA
Over 1600 of the Best Fly Patterns
Edited by Al & Gretchen Beatty

Simply stated, this book is a Federation of Fly Fishers' conclave taken to the next level, a level that allows the reader to enjoy the learning and sharing in the comfort of their own home. The flies, ideas, and techniques shared herein are from the "best of the best" demonstration fly tiers North America has to offer. The tiers are the famous as well as the unknown with one simple characteristic in common; they freely share their knowledge. Many of the unpublished patterns in this book contain materials, tips, tricks, or gems of information never before seen.

As you leaf through these pages, you will get from them just what you would if you spent time in the fly tying area at any FFF function. At such a show, if you dedicate time to observing the individual tiers, you can learn the information, tips, or tricks they are demonstrating. All of this knowledge can be found in *Federation of Fly Fishers Fly Pattern Encyclopedia* so get comfortable and get ready to improve upon your fly tying technique with the help of some of North America's best fly tiers. Full color, 8 1/2 x 11 inches, 232 pages.
SB: $39.95   ISBN: 1-57188-208-1
SPIRAL HB: $49.95   ISBN: 1-57188-209-X

NYMPH FLY-TYING TECHNIQUES
Jim Schollmeyer

Noted photographer and author, Jim Schollmeyer, now puts his talents to tying nymphs. More than just a book of nymph patterns, this book takes a different approach. Realizing that many nymph patterns have evolved from variations on a handful of basic designs and tying techniques, Jim has written on these evolutions and how your repertoire of flies can be broadened by seeing how a variety of modifications can be worked into fly designs to produce the desired appearance or behavior.

With his crisp step-by-step photos and concise text, Jim Schollmeyer has done it again, another great fly-tying technique book. Full-color, 8 1/2 x 11 inches, 125 pages.
SB: $23.95   ISBN: 1-57188-266-9
SPIRAL HB: $43.00   ISBN: 1-57188-267-7

FLY PATTERNS FOR STILLWATERS
Philip Rowley

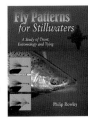

Phil has spent countless hours at lakes studying the food sources that make up the diet of trout; then set up home aquariums to more closely observe the movement, development, and emergence of the aquatic insects. In this book he explains the link between understanding the food base within lakes to designing effective fly patterns for these environs. Phil covers all major trout food sources for the whole year. He gives detailed information on each, plus how to tie a representative pattern and fish it effectively. Numerous proven stillwater patterns are given for each insect and include clear and concise tying instructions. This book will be a long-standing stillwater fly pattern reference for years to come. All-color, 8 1/2 x 11 inches, 104 pages.
SB: $29.95   ISBN: 1-57188-195-6

STEELHEAD DREAMS
The Theory, Method, Science and Madness of Great Lakes Steelhead Fly Fishing
Matt Supinski

Screaming runs, big, thrashing jumps, relentless power—it's no wonder steelheading is an obsession for so many anglers. In *Steelhead Dreams*, Matt shares all you need to become a better steelhead fly fisherman, including: steelhead biology and habitat; reading and mastering the waters where they thrive; steelhead habits; techniques for all four seasons; effective presentations; tackle; plus best fly styles, casting tips, Great Lakes steelhead fisheries, tying tips, and so much more. If you are addicted to steelhead or look forward to becoming so, you must read this book to learn all you need to know about this wondrous fish and the techniques for catching them. Full color, 8 1/2 x 11 inches, 144 pages.
SB: $29.95   ISBN: 1-57188-219-7
HB: $39.95   ISBN: 1-57188-258-8

TROUT FLIES OF THE EAST
Best Contemporary Patterns from East of the Rocky Mountains
Jim Schollmeyer and Ted Leeson

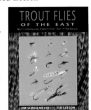

In fly-fishinging, there is no substitute for local knowledge. Walk into any fly shop and you will find "shop patterns"—flies local to the area. Far more often than not, these are the top choices for fishing rivers and lakes in a given area. Second in a series devoted to celebrating these flies, this book focuses on trout flies, although some are well-suited to steelhead, salmon, and warmwater species as well. Patterns shared include: attractors and multi-purpose; mayflies; caddisflies; stoneflies; midges; damsel and dragonfly, hellgrammite, crustaceans; baitfish; leeches; terrestrials; and more. Once again, Jim and Ted provide top-quality writing and photography. Your fly-fishing library is not complete without this first-rate book. 8 1/2 x 11 inches; 128 pages. All color.
SB: $34.95   ISBN: 1-57188-196-4
SPIRAL HB: $44.95   ISBN: 1-57188-197-2

Ask for these books at your local fishing or book store or order from:
1-800-541-9498 (8 to 5 p.s.t.) • www.amatobooks.com
Frank Amato Publications, Inc. • P.O. Box 82112 • Portland, Oregon 97282